Twayne's English Authors Series

EDITOR OF THIS VOLUME

Kinley E. Roby

Northeastern University

James Cousins

TEAS 280

Pencil Sketch by Florence Gillespie

James Cousins

JAMES COUSINS

By WILLIAM A. DUMBLETON

State University of New York, Albany

TWAYNE PUBLISHERS

A DIVISION OF G. K. HALL & CO., BOSTON

Published in 1980 by Twayne Publishers,
A Division of G. K. Hall & Co.
All Rights Reserved

Printed on permanent/durable acid-free paper and bound
in the United States of America

First Printing

Library of Congress Cataloging in Publication Data

Dumbleton, William A
James Cousins.

(Twayne's English authors series : TEAS 280)
Bibliography: p. 136 - 41
Includes index.
1.   Cousins, James Henry, 1873 - 1956—
Criticism and interpretation.   2.   Theosophy.
PR6005.082Z63   821'.9'12   79-20906
ISBN 0-8057-6745-2

Contents

About the Author

William A. Dumbleton is Associate Professor of English and Direc-
tor of Undergraduate Study in English at the State University of
New York at Albany. He earned his B.A. and M.A. at SUNYA, his
Ph.D. at the University of Pennsylvania. Professor Dumbleton has
lived and studied in Ireland, where he earned an M.A. in Anglo-
Irish Literature with First Class Honors from University College,
Dublin. He also taught at the American University in Cairo, Egypt.
The author of a number of articles on Irish and English literature,
he is the editor of James Cousins' plays, *The Sleep of the King* and
The Sword of Dermot (Irish Drama Series, DePaul University,
Chicago, 1973). A member of the American Committee for Irish
Studies and of the Canadian Association for Irish Studies, Professor
Dumbleton also serves as a member of the Executive Committee
and as the United States Treasurer for the International Association
for the Study of Anglo-Irish Literature.

Preface

James Cousins was an interesting and significant poet and playwright from Ulster. A catalytic figure and participant in Dublin in the Irish Literary Renaissance, he was called "the voice of the North" at the time of the Revival; *The Nation* in London said, "artistically Mr. Cousins can only be put below the two leaders of his movement (AE and W. B. Yeats)." He was instrumental in bringing together in 1902 the Fay brothers, their acting group, and AE to stage a first performance of two plays: Russell's play *Deirdre*, featuring Cousins and Padraic Colum in the cast; and Yeats' *Cathleen ni Houlihan,* starring Maud Gonne in the title role. Thus, with the union of Irish actors and Irish plays, was Irish theater established. Cousins went on to write several plays for the Irish theater while he was in Ireland, and he continued as a prolific poet for the rest of his life.

Like Yeats and Russell, Cousins was interested in Oriental thought, but his attraction to Theosophy, and his association with Madame Blavatsky and Annie Besant, drew him to the Theosophical Headquarters in Madras, India, in 1915. Apart from considerable travel, Cousins remained in India until his death in 1956, dedicating himself to poetry, the arts, and Theosophical causes.

A productive writer of many volumes of verse, several plays, some interesting volumes of prose and criticism, and a combined autobiography with his wife, Cousins has not been examined in a critical volume, though his name appears in passing in some studies, and his verse continues to appear in representative anthologies of Irish verse. Two of his plays, *The Sleep of the King* and *The Sword of Dermot,* were published in 1973 by DePaul University in its Irish Drama Series, and his play, *The Racing Lug,* appears in *Lost Plays of the Irish Renaissance,* edited in 1970 by Robert Hogan and James Kilroy. Anyone interested in Cousins and his works owes an enormous debt, as do I, to Alan Denson for his prodigiously complete, *James H. Cousins and Margaret E. Cousins: A Bio-Bibliographical Survey.* All study of Cousins must begin there.

This volume is a critical study of Cousins and his writings, though some of his presumably lesser essays in India have not been available to me. The opening chapter surveys Cousins' life from the early years in Belfast and through his fifteen years in Dublin and over forty years in India. Other than in his autobiography there is only scant material on Cousins' life available elsewhere.

Theosophical thought is the heart of all of Cousins' writing, just as it was the foundation of his life for his mature years. Chapter Two is, first, a distillation and presentation of Cousins' Theosophical thinking as it relates to and provides clarification for his written works. The prose works, most of which are patently Theosophical in nature, are also treated in Chapter Two.

Chapter Three is a consideration and evaluation of Cousins' plays. The majority of them were written in Dublin, but Cousins returned briefly to playwriting in India and occasionally turned to the Irish myths for subject matter.

Chapter Four is a critical survey of the verse, considering the forms, techniques, and subject matter that emerge from the verse. While always essentially Theosophical in utterance, Cousins was a poet of considerable range in form and technique. Much of Cousins' verse consists of narratives of Irish mythological stories. But his basic ability is a lyric gift, and it is the lyric that best represents his continuing talent in Ireland and India, a talent that Cousins saw as rooted in his Celtic imagination.

The closing chapter is an assessment of the literary relevance of this lesser but significant thinker, playwright, and poet.

I am indebted to Roger McHugh of University College, Dublin, for first pointing out to me the unfortunate limbo into which Cousins had been cast; and to Alan Denson, for his guidance in studying Cousins and for his essential bibliographical survey. The pursuit of Cousins' writings has put me in debt to the resources and the kind help of the Library of University College, Dublin; the Library of Trinity College, Dublin; the National Library of Ireland; the Library of the Dublin Theosophical Society; and, in the United States, the libraries of Brown University, University of California, University of Delaware, Harvard University, Miami University (Oxford, Ohio), State University of New York at Albany, State Library of New York, City of New York Library, University of Pennsylvania, and University of Washington. The Research Foundation of the State University of New York helped by granting me a Summer Fellowship and thereby providing some time for working on this study. I owe also a satisfying debt to my students over the years, most especially to those in my Irish literature courses, for their stimulus in the classroom that helps to bring about and sustain scholarly effort.

I am particularly appreciative of the kind permission to quote from the works of James Cousins granted to me by Smt. Rukmini Devi Arundale, the Literary Executor of the works of James Cousins, from the Kalakshetra, Tiruvanmiyur, Madras, India, and kindly communicated to me by K. Sankara Menon, the Executor of Cousins' will, also at the Kalakshetra.

WILLIAM A. DUMBLETON

State University of New York, Albany

Chronology

James Henry Sproull Cousins (occasional pseudonyms:
Henry Sproull, Seumas Ó'Cuisín)

1873	22 July. Born at No. 18, Cavour Street, Belfast, Ireland.
1894	*Ben Madighan and Other Poems.*
1895	Became member of Gaelic League in Belfast.
1897	Moved to Dublin in May, subsequently met George Russell, W. B. Yeats, and Fay Brothers. *The Legend of the Blemished King and Other Poems.*
1900	*The Voice of One.*
1902	In April, acted in AE's *Deirdre*, first publicly performed with Yeats' *Cathleen ni Houlihan.* In October, first performances of *The Sleep of the King* and *The Racing Lug*, by Irish National Dramatic Company.
1903	Married, on April 9, Margaret E. Gillespie, from Boyle, Roscommon, in the Sandymount Methodist Church. In April, first performance of *The Sword of Dermot.*
1905	In August, began teaching in The High School, Dublin. Subjects: English Literature and, subsequently, Geography.
1906	*The Quest.*
1907	*The Awakening.*
1908	In May, joined the Theosophical Society in London and aided in formation of Dublin Branch. *The Bell Branch.*
1912	*Etain the Beloved and Other Poems.* Trip to Normandy. *The Wisdom of the West: An Introduction to the Interpretative Study of Irish Mythology;*
1913	*The Bases of Theosophy.* Moved to Liverpool in June, to work for a vegetarian food company.
1915	*Straight and Crooked.* Sailed for India in October, to work for the Theosophical Society at the International Headquarters at Adyar, Madras, as literary sub-editor of a paper, *New India.*

1916   Began teaching at Theosophical College at Madanapalle, in July.

1917   *New Ways in English Literature.* Appointed vice-principal of Theosophical College at Madanapalle. *The Kingdom of Youth: Essays Towards National Education; The Garland of Life: Poems West and East.*

1918   *The Renaissance in India.* Appointed principal of Theosophical College at Madanapalle.

1919   *Ode to Truth; The King's Wife. Moulted Feathers; Footsteps of Freedom: Essays.*

1919 -   Guest professor of Modern English Poetry at Kei-
1920   ogijuku University, Tokyo, Japan. Lectures subsequently published in 1921, entitled *Modern English Poetry: Its Characteristics and Tendencies.* Received Honarary Doctorate from University in 1923.

1920   *Sea-Change.* Returned to principalship of Theosophical College at Madanapalle.

1921   *The Play of Brahma: An Essay on Drama in National Revival.*

1922   *Surya-Gita (Sun Songs),* for Rabindranath Tagore. *Work and Worship: Essays on Culture and Creative Art.* Became director of studies of Brahmavidyashrama (School of Universal Study) at Adyar, Madras.

1923   *The New Japan: Impressions and Reflections; Modern Indian Artists.*

1925   European trip, from March to August, with a visit to Ireland. *The Social Value of Arts and Crafts; Samadarsana [Synthetic vision]: A Study in Indian Psychology; The Philosophy of Beauty: A Western Survey and an Eastern Contribution; Forest Meditation and Other Poems; Heathen Essays.*

1926   *Above the Rainbow and Other Poems; A Tibetan Banner.*

1927   *The Sword of Dermot.*

1928   *The Shrine and Other Poems.* Trip around the world, April - October.

1929   *The Girdle: Poems.*

1930   Leaves in April for Europe and United States to lecture.

1931 -   Guest Lecturer in Modern English Poetry in Col-
1932   lege of the City of New York.

1932   *A Wandering Harp: Selected Poems.*

1932 -   "Literary year" from July to March spent on Capri; Gretta in India.

1933   Returned to India. Appointed Principal, Besant Theosophical College at Madanapalle. *The Work Promethean: Interpretations and Applications of Shelley's Poetry; A Study in Synthesis; A Bardic Pilgrimage:* Second Selection of Poetry.

1934   Appointed a part-time advisor to the Government of Travancore.

1937   Admitted into Hindu worship. Travelled to Bali and Java. Put in charge of Government Museum, Trivandrum.

1938   *The Oracle and Other Poems.* Resigned as Principal of Besant College. Appointed Art Advisor to Government of Travancore, on a full-time basis.

1940   *Collected Poems.*

1941   *The Faith of the Artist.*

1942   *The Hound of Uladh: Two Plays in Verse.*

1946   *Reflections Before Sunset: Poems.*

1948   Appointment ended as Art Advisor to Government of Travancore. Became Vice-President of Kalakshetra, an academy of the arts at Adyar.

1949   *Twenty-Four Sonnets.*

1950   *We Two Together,* combined autobiography with wife.

1954   Margaret Cousins died, March 11.

1956   Died on February 20 at Madanapalle; remains cremated.

CHAPTER 1

Biographical Background

" MY forbears . . . came to live in me"[1] is the expression
James Cousins chose to express the fact of his birth on July
22nd, 1873 as the son of working-class Wesleyan Methodist parents
amid the religious enmities of Belfast. Reaction against the religious
narrowness and bigotry in his upbringing and background
strengthened enormously as Cousins matured, and this repulsion,
somewhat in the manner of Yeats' reaction against his atheistic early
upbringing, sent Cousins on a lifelong spiritual odyssey, which
brought him to Theosophy, Hinduism, and a continuing repudiation
of any specific theological externals or the dogma of any one
faith, and to strong belief that spiritual truth was to be found in all
religions. The narrow view that Cousins found as he looked back on
his early works appalled him:

What gives me cold shivers . . . is the religious ideas that appear to have
governed my thought and expression at nineteen: heaven for the 'saved'
(the Wesleyan Methodists and perhaps a few other brands of Protestants),
hell for the 'lost' (all Papists and some not too good Protestants). (31)

The expansion and broadening of a religious and philosophical
point of view became the main governing impulse of Cousins' life
and the main axis of the greater part of his creative efforts in verse
and drama in his years in Ireland. He found his own intuitive interpretations and beliefs within the myths of Ireland and shaped his
creative utterances accordingly, finding in Irish mythology his own
cosmic awareness:

The personalities and events of the Irish mythos became to me the imaginative incarnations of powers and processes in the universe and myself. I
felt that vision was more ultimate than insight and more prophetic than
foresight; and through its contemplation and embodiment in my early
poems I aspired towards the capacity to see the significance of the insignificant and to feel the eternal in the temporal.[2]

I *Ulster*

Cousins' foundation in formal schooling was far from strong. He completed regular classes at the age of twelve and then undertook a series of menial jobs while he learned shorthand and typewriting. These skills brought him to new levels of employment; he taught shorthand and typing in the Belfast Mercantile Academy, was private secretary and speech writer for the Mayor of Belfast, and also served as editor of the *Irish Phonographic Bulletin*.

But the end of formal academic training did not close the door to Cousins' personal pursuit of knowledge. His own literary interest brought him to the verse of Swinburne, AE's *Homeward Songs by the Way*, and Yeats' "The Wanderings of Oisin." Subsequently he joined the Gaelic League, without telling family or friends. His attendance at the ceremonies of the Robert Burns centenary moved him to write a poem about it, and subsequently, at nineteen, the press published one of his poems about a statue of Burns, to publicize the need for funds to pay the bill for the statue. (The campaign was a success.)

A painting by John Vinycomb, "The Rout of Mac Gillmore on Ben Madighan," sent Cousins to Samuel Ferguson's *Corby Mac Gillmore* for information and, consequently, to the mountain Ben Madighan near Belfast. There, on the site described in an ancient story of the confrontation of Christianity with a pagan clan, he contemplated the event and celebrated it in his first narrative poem, "Ben Madighan." This poem was published with others in 1894. Soon after, a group of six verse writers, including Cousins, was formed; its members selfconsciously named it the Kit Kat Club, and in its short existence produced a book of their efforts, *Sung by Six*, in 1896.

Inspired by his reading of Irish stories in Ferguson, and by his own writing about Ben Madighan, Cousins now began writing poems drawn from stories, legends, or associations with particular nearby places, notably "The Legend of St. Makea of Endrim." Soon after, in 1897, feeling he had grown beyond his family and Belfast, he took a job in Dublin. He was then twenty-four.

II *Dublin and Marriage*

Dublin brought its series of jobs: he was a reporter to the Royal Academy of Medicine and a teacher of Geography and English Literature at the High School on Harcourt Street, a sizable number of whose graduates went to Trinity College. As a teacher, he wrote two geography textbooks and edited two high-school-level literature textbooks. He also became the unpaid secretary of the newly organized Maunsel and Company, book publishers. This brought him in touch with Dublin literary figures. Most important, in the climate of Dublin he continued to write verse and he began to write plays.

In 1899, Cousins met Margaret E. Gillespie, a student and teacher of music. They were married on April 9, 1903, in Sandymount Methodist Church. This union was to have a profound influence on the life and future works of the poet. For Cousins, Gretta's declaration on their wedding day that she would join him in his vegetarianism was "an invisible marriage, deeper and more binding than the ritual of conventional respectability." (81) Together, following their beliefs, the couple sought experience in psychic phenomena. Before his marriage, Cousins had already become interested, mainly through his fellow poet and playwright, George Russell, in the idea of reincarnation. Cousins disliked the idea until "one morning walking to a tram-stop on my way from my lodgings to the office, thinking of things far removed from reincarnation, I suddenly saw myself as myself coming from myself, through the gate of death, to myself. I recognized paternal and maternal transmissions in characteristics of body, mind, and feeling, but saw my-self as the spectator and user of these, modifying them according to the genius and purpose of my real self." (67-68)

Through Russell, too, Cousins had come to study the occult and had come under the influence of the Theosophist Madame Blavatsky and her basic work, *Secret Doctrine*, and had come to know the Bengali visitor to Dublin, Mohini Chaterjee; he also knew of AE's personal experience in extensions of consciousness. Margaret Cousins, with James' help, immersed herself in the psychic and occult. According to the Cousins, at this time Margaret began to function as a medium. Primarily through automatic writing and a moving planchette (with occasional clairaudience and clairvoyance), Margaret believed that she received directions, inspirations, and interpretations from the psychic realm. Not surprisingly, the couple soon shared their experiences and their beliefs with their poet friend, William Butler Yeats, and with Maud Gonne and several others concurrently interested in the occult. Occasionally they attended séances together. On one particular evening with a medium who was a stranger to Yeats and Maud Gonne, all those present claim to have seen a spirit appearing behind Yeats, "a straight, tall, bearded man, over whom a flag connected with Ireland flew." Then as a picture of a pig seemed to appear, the voice of the medium announced enigmatically, "This pig has shot himself." Subsequent interpretation of the two visions relied upon information beyond the knowledge of the medium or the assembled group to determine that the tall gentleman was Parnell and that the pig represented Parnell's connection with a forger, Piggott, who had accused Parnell of crime in a London newspaper. Parnell had brought the newspaper to court, and Piggott (the pig who shot himself) had been a suicide. (121 - 22)

According to the Cousins' reports, Margaret, more usually called Gretta, also received biblical interpretations for herself, drawn in a remote and detailed Persian fashion of which her conscious mind was in ignorance. From a Dublin lecture by Theosophist Annie Besant, entitled "Theosophy and Ireland," James began to see an especial relevance to the communications he and Gretta were receiving. "I gathered the idea that clairvoyance, or revelation, or both, declared a long process of racial and cultural evolution out of which Ireland was ultimately to emerge as the spiritual mentor of Europe, even as India had long been to Asia." (74 - 75) Thus for Cousins, his writings and his Theosophical beliefs merged and he saw—like Yeats—a somewhat priestly mission for himself as an Irish author.

Margaret's receptive powers, no doubt sensitive to the Irish Literary movement of the time, began to envision stories of ancient Celtic material. While in what she described as a trance or dreamlike state, scenes, actions, and symbols which were totally foreign to her consciousness would appear to her. When she awakened she would describe the scenes and symbols and narrate the stories to her husband, who would use them as the seedlings for his poetry. Cousins claimed that her inspirations frequently strained his poetic craft, but on occasion her trances provided him precisely the right material.

For example, Cousins' "The Marriage of Lir and Niav" contains a scene of the queen ascending her throne in a great hall as harpers played for a birthday celebration. The scene with all its embellishments came directly from Gretta's "higher consciousness." Cousins had been laboring under the strain of expression for this scene when Gretta awakened from a trance with the solution to his quandary. He describes the scene in their dual autobiography, *We Two Together,* of Gretta in the vision

. . . having reached the plain on which the Irish Deities, the De Danaans, dwelt. Each enthroned God was accompanied by his Goddess. One of the latter came towards her carrying something like a casket in her hands. As the Goddess came nearer, Gretta knelt in reverence. The Goddess told her to rise and look in the casket. Side by side were a large ruby and an equally large pearl. Gretta asked the Goddess to open her understanding. The Goddess said: "The ruby is my husband, Lir. The Pearl is myself, Niav. Remember this when you return to your world, and tell it to Jim: he will understand." I [James] understood; for while the "magnetic sleep" had been proceeding I had been working on the poem in another room. A double figure of speech came into my mind and I had much imaginative delight in shaping it into lines; pearl for Niav and a ruby for Lir. Symbolically the pearl was the inner spiritual core of life, the ruby the executive mind. The two together represented the perfect unit, superhuman and human. (123)

Cousins' early volume of verse, *The Quest* (1906), dedicated to Margaret, contained "myth-poems . . . received in outline psychically" (133). Both James and Gretta Cousins took up membership in the Theosophical Society in London in 1908, and Mrs. Annie Besant, president of the International Society after the death of her converter, Madame Blavatsky, chose Gretta to form a branch of the Society in Dublin. This Gretta did, and the Society survives today. Their marriage, James and Gretta felt, was distinctive as a "persistent joint search into the realities involved in birth and life and death" and "mutual in our physical and mental disciplines." Both believed that consciousness "could operate apart from its physical instrument" and therefore could survive physical embodiment. (111) Gretta, in extension of this belief, felt the realities of sex and of human birth were shocking and degrading and that the evolution of form must substitute "some more artistic way of continuance of the race" (109).

Gretta was spirited in other ways as well and was a devoted and sometimes militant suffragette. Cousins' joined her in her endeavors. In his relationship with Gretta, Cousins felt that she was "destined to broaden me into real manhood by stimulating in me the reactions of latent womanhood, and for whom I was to do a complementary service." (81) With this unifying link, they both devoted themselves to women's rights. In addition to dedicated, peaceful educational campaigning and marching in Ireland and England in behalf of votes for women, Gretta resorted to controlled violence on two occaions. In November of 1910 a group of suffragettes, Gretta included, wished to hand the Prime Minister a resolution of protest at 10 Downing Street. Home Secretary Winston Churchill gave an order to the London police: the group was to be "put out of action." Churchill's order resulted in one hundred and nineteen women arrested, fifty in need of medical attention for injuries caused by police action. Gretta's indignation brought her and a few other women quietly to 10 Downing Street that midnight. They threw potatoes and pieces of flower pots (Gretta's choice) through the windows and were arrested; Gretta was held for a month in Holloway Jail. Similarly in 1913, in protest against the proposed Home Rule Bill which excluded women's votes, Gretta and two other women militantly smashed windows in Dublin Castle, primarily to win wide publicity for their cause. This arrest resulted in just that, as well as in another one-month jail sentence, this time a short while in Mountjoy Prison and the remainder in Tullamore Prison. While in Tullamore Prison, she staged a hunger strike. Gretta's cause, with which Cousins was in sympathy and in which he was very active, motivated a few poems stating his belief. Gretta's imprisonment and release motivated verse commemoration also. It was soon after Gretta's release from Tullamore that the Cousins left Ireland in 1913.

Among the literary friendships of the Cousins in Dublin was one with James Joyce, who used Gretta's name for Gabriel Conroy's wife in his major story, "The Dead."[3] Joyce and Gretta had music as a common interest:

James Joyce was a favourite of mine though he was reputed to be a "bad boy." I delighted in his lovely tenor voice especially when I accompanied some of his Irish songs with nobody but ourselves to hear in our little drawing room. (106)

Joseph Holloway mentions Joyce dropping in to the Cousins' house, where there were "always interesting people"; he thought Joyce a "mysterious kind of youth with weird penetrating eyes . . . a strange boy; I cannot fathom him."[4] The Cousins were kind to Joyce, offering him lodging when he was broke, but by then they had become complete and evangelical vegetarians, and Joyce left the vegetarian household in a few days complaining of stomach difficulties caused by a "typhoid turnip."[5] Joyce later stayed again for two days but left, unable to tolerate what Professor Ellmann calls the "do-good household."[6] Joyce later wrote of James Cousins in his 1912 broadside entitled "Gas From a Burner":

> I printed the table-book of Cousins
> Though (asking your pardon) as for the verse
> 'Twould give you a heartburn in your arse.

III   *Theatrical Activities*

Despite this blunt dismissal of Cousins' work by Joyce, Cousins, while continuing to write verse, had undoubtedly performed great service to the Irish theater in its early years. From the moment he arrived in Dublin, Cousins had observed and been interested in the theater, but he was appalled and disappointed by its overall English nature. He was particularly distressed that the actors were all English.

In June, 1901, Cousins met W. B. Yeats, who was to become a dominant theatrical force. Detecting Cousins' interest in theater, Yeats appointed him to the committee for the third season of the Irish Literary Theatre, the season which produced Douglas Hyde's play in Gaelic, *The Twisting of the Rope*. That November, Cousins also saw the small acting group of the brothers Willie and Frank Fay, the Ormond Dramatic Society. It was Cousins who was instrumental in bringing the two groups together—the Irish Literary Theatre with its interest in Irish plays, and the Fay brothers' group with its interest in Irish acting. When together, the groups formed the foundation of the later development of the Abbey Theatre. Cousins, in conversation with Frank Fay, asked if Fay would be interested in Irish plays, and in answer to Fay's question, "Where are the plays?" (66), Cousins drew attention to the early part of AE's *Deirdre*, based on the Irish legend, which he knew AE had partially completed. W. G. Fay felt it "was beautifully written in a lyrical prose that was easy to speak. I said to Frank, 'Here is an Irish play that I would not mind trying to produce with our Ormond Dramatic Society'."[7] Cousins brought the Fays to AE's house and together they persuaded him to finish the play and turn it over to the group for production. Frank Fay subsequently asked Cousins to play the part of Ainnle and the Irish writer Padraic Colum to play Buinne in the initial production. Since the cast was larger than the Ormond Society's membership, W. G. Fay formed a new society *ad hoc* called W. G. Fay's Irish National Dramatic Company. Cousins was a member of this group. While *Deirdre* was in rehearsal, Frank Fay met Yeats, Lady Gregory, and Maud Gonne, and told them of the play. Yeats offered his play, *Cathleen ni Houlihan,* to them if *Deirdre* was too short to fill the evening. As it turned out, it was, so the Fays decided to produce the two plays as a double bill. Miss Gonne joined the company to play the role of Cathleen on the successful opening on April 2, 3, and 4, 1902, in the Hall of St. Theresa's Total Abstinence Association in Clarendon Street.

The opening has been assessed by Ernest Boyd as an important one:

This production of *Deirdre* was the beginning of a movement that not only created a native drama in Ireland, but afterwards stimulated both Scotland and Wales to follow . . . It gave to the Gael that which had never before existed in the history of the race — a means of expressing the national consciousness through the medium of drama.[8]

Thus Cousins' foresight and initiative were integral components in the exciting beginnings of national theater. And although his own evaluation of the event is perhaps excessive, his action was worthy of note and praise:

Presumably the Time Spirit would have found persons through whom to carry out its intention if I had been elsewhere when Frank Fay called at the office of a coal and shipping company [where Cousins was working] in D'olier Street, Dublin, and a few minutes' chat, made me the father and him the mother of Irish drama in its real family circle. (96)

In any case, the success of the undertaking urged Frank Fay to hope that productions would continue. One evening, while making up Cousins for his role in *Deirdre,* Fay asked Cousins to write a play for the group. Days later, on Sunday morning, April 13, 1902, an incident from Cousins' boyhood involving a boat with a large sail called a racing lug so seized him that he wrote his realistic play, *The Racing Lug,* in a matter of hours, actually so "inspired" that he believed he really had "transcribed" the play from a voice outside himself. When Yeats saw the rough draft on the next day, he proclaimed the play perfect with no need of further work; the following week it went into rehearsal.

Frank Fay was at this time also concerned with insuring high caliber performance on the part of the company. In hopes of getting a blank verse play to develop the acting group, Frank Fay suggested to Cousins the Irish story of Prince Connla and the fairy maiden, who called Connla to the Land of the Ever Young. Cousins accepted the suggestion; the result was his play, *The Sleep of the King.* In writing this play, Cousins saw that his mind "had moved from a level of consciousness different from the realism of 'The Racing Lug.' I had reached the interpretative view of life and its movement from spiritual origins to spiritual fulfillment; in other words, had found a mode of expression for an inborn intuitive relationship of my inner self with the nature and technique of the universe." (72 - 73) This play too was to serve as a vehicle for continuing the momentum of the movement for a national voice.

The Irish National Theatre Society was formed in April from this theatrical group. Yeats was chosen as president with Maud Gonne, George Russell, and Douglas Hyde as vice presidents. W. G. Fay was the stage manager; members included Cousins, F. J. Fay, and Padraic Colum. The first production of the group on October 29, 1902 was Cousins' *The Sleep of the King,* followed two nights later by his *The Racing Lug.* For protection against his employers, who disapproved of the theater, Cousins used for each play the *nom de plume* Seumas Ó'Cuisín. *The Racing Lug* later played at the opening of the Ulster Literary Theatre in Belfast. Of *The Sleep of the King,* Yeats said to Cousins, "Splendid, my boy, splendid. Beautiful verse beautifully spoken by native actors. Just what we wanted." The last sentence, with its patronizing air, gave the company a twinge, Cousins felt, with its "suggestion that we were contributory to him and not he to us" (76). Yeats' comments to Cousins and his encouragement of his early efforts indicate that he apparently had at the outset recognized value in Cousins' work. Documentation of this can be found in the notes of others. Frank Fay records Yeats' writing to him in April 1902 during the early formation of the group, "I think we must work in some such way, getting all the good plays we can from Cousins and Russell and anybody else, but carrying out our theories of the stage as rigorously as possible."[9] Nonetheless, by the latter part of 1902, after reading Cousins' new play, *Sold,* Yeats wrote to Lady Gregory,

I have written Fay a very severe letter about Cousins' play *Sold* in U. I. [*Sold* published on December 27, 1902 in *United Irishman,* and cited as "the first real comedy of Irish life" by the editor, Arthur Griffith]. They talk about doing it but I have told him that it is "rubbish and vulgar rubbish." I have wound up by saying that I did not mark the letter private—he might show it if he liked. Cousins is evidently hopeless and the sooner I have him as an enemy the better. I think Fay will see from my letter that, although I do not interfere with their freedom to produce what they like, too much Cousins would make work in common out of the question.[10]

About a year later, Yeats wrote to Lily Yeats that he and others "did snuff out" Cousins.[11] Cousins used similar terminology in his autobiography: "The rest of us, not excluding AE, were snuffed out" (77). There is no further clarification of the cause of Yeats' newly-developed disapproval of Cousins. Very likely, the need for working harmony in the small theatrical group was disturbed by the clash of Cousins' ego and vocal enthusiasms with Yeats' plans for development of the Irish theater. The immediate issue was, to be sure, Cousins' poor farce, *Sold*. Neither the quality nor the *genre* suited Yeats.

After the split with Yeats and the theatrical group led by Yeats, Cousins wrote two more plays. Cousins' play, *The Sword of Dermot*, was first produced on April 20, 1903, by another group, the National Literary Society; and his play, *A Man's Foes*, was staged on November 3, 1903. *Sold*, the play which had troubled Yeats, was produced in Cork City, in December, 1905, but Cousins' interest in writing drama in Ireland had waned and it ended with this production.

IV *Verse and Other Literary Activities*

Cousins' interest in verse-writing, however, continued throughout his years in Dublin; during those sixteen years, he published six volumes of poetry and numerous individual poems in periodicals. By the publication in Dublin of *The Voice of One* in 1900, he felt he had "passed out of the stage of juvenilia" (58), and the subsequent volumes reveal a growing range and ability in form and technique. Irish subject matter and myth, with its possibilities for spiritual intensities, continued as his primary concern. He was sometimes referred to in these years as the third poet, after Yeats and AE, of the Renaissance in Ireland, and a significant poetic voice from the North. Like Yeats and AE, Cousins continued to be drawn to "other-worldly," unifying elements. As guests at a dinner in 1912 in Maud Gonne's house in Normandy, James and Gretta Cousins were introduced to *Gitanjali* by the Indian poet, Rabindranath Tagore. Cousins said:

Their simple profundities and exaltations reached depths and heights beyond the bearings of race and country and language. We knew (at any rate I did) why Jubainville, the French scholar, found parallels between the old Celtic religion and the religion of India, and why an Irish Goddess was cured of a legendary illness (as told in a seventh century record in Irish of an older tradition) by drinking the milk of two cows that two Irish Gods on a journey had brought from India, the milk being recommended because India was "a land of righteousness." We were one in spirit, we pioneers of the new Irish movement in poetry, and the poet from India. And to those who are one in spirit, the dissimilarities of expression are even more generous in suggestion of the spiritual through the material, which is the essence of mysticism in arts, than the similarities that the archaeological mind values. [12]

Cousins' admiration for Tagore was to continue for the remainder of his life. And at that early meeting, when both poets were involved in the early stirrings of nationalistic sentiment and determination, the similarly spiritual quality of Tagore's efforts must have greatly moved Cousins. These lines from one of the poems of *Gitanjali*, for example, would most certainly have tapped a fertile vein in Cousins' mind, for they contain both rebellion against constriction and yearning for absorption.

> Where the world has not been broken up into
> fragments by narrow domestic walls;
> Where words come out from the depth of truth;
> Where tireless striving stretches its arms
> towards perfection;
> Where the clear stream of reason has not lost
> its way into the dreary desert sand of
> dead habit;
> Where the mind is led forward by thee into
> ever-widening thought and action —
> Into that heaven of freedom, my Father, let
> my country awake. [13]

Whether it was that poem or some other, Tagore's poetry moved Cousins greatly. For Cousins was not a dilettante clinging to the literary movement as to a mode. He was intensely serious of purpose, and he felt the call to be a part of the enormously important and beautiful resurgence to life of the Celtic spirit. He was a man propelled by a spiritual mission. The evening with Tagore merely furthered his zeal and caused him to verbalize his desire.

There was something to be sung, and a way of singing it . . . My born wish was to feel the palm of my hand and all that it symbolised, held in the sure grasp of infinity, a dedicated instrument to be used by the creative spirit that I felt to be the aesthetical cause and intellectual explanation of life. (216 - 17)

In addition to dramatic and poetic work, Cousins had a brief career as a periodical editor. One of the founders, in February, 1911, of the little review, *The Pioneer*, Cousins was also the literary editor. The stated object in the first issue of the magazine was:

to stimulate, organise and make articulate a growing body of thought which . . . is striving towards the elevation and enrichment of life . . . This policy is based on the affirmation of the fundamental unity, interdependence, and continuity of the apparently diverse activities of mankind.

Cousins no doubt helped to compose this statement. The few issues of the magazine contained poems and essays of Cousins, sometimes under the pseudonym Henry Sproull. The last issue was published in April 1911, two months after the magazine's inception.

After *The Pioneer* ceased, Cousins and Francis Sheehy-Skeffington, with whom Cousins and Gretta had been active in the Irish Women's Franchise League, founded and co-edited *The Irish Citizen*, a weekly paper promoting women's rights. Cousins' efforts here were shortlived, since he and Gretta sailed for Liverpool from Dublin on June 2, 1913, en route to India. Cousins intended to work for a vegetarian food concern in India, but by the time he arrived there, he had accepted an editorship with the Theosophical Society, whose international headquarters were in Madras. Cousins received many tributes, on leaving Ireland, the most significant of which was a special performance of *The Racing Lug* and *The Sleep of the King*. In addition, he was praised as a poet, fighter for women's rights, student of religion, and food reformer. Padraic Colum cited him for introducing the humanity of the North to the South, and for showing in his excellent verse the "powers which spiritually moved under the visible surface of human life."[14] *The Irish Citizen* continued to be published until 1916, when Sheehy-Skeffington was murdered.

V *To India*

Though the Cousins' trip from Ireland to India was a long one—the war causing a two-year delay in Liverpool, England—the move was spiritually an easy one. Cousins had found his own center of spiritual beliefs in Ireland, and through Irish mythology had elaborated his own view of the relationship of temporal physical realities to eternal spiritual essence. This view remained with him for the rest of his life; he never lost his philosophy that life was evolving to the spiritual perfection of its origin. Developed solidly in Ireland, his Theosophical view became the foundation of Cousins' approach to India and the pith of his literary utterances there. He had come to his mode of thinking, he saw clearly, by way of the Irish Literary Renaissance:

Up to 1913, when I left Ireland—to become as afterwards appeared, a world wanderer, gathering nomadic riches, but squandering the marketable possibilities of a settled abode—the vision and enthusiasm of the movement that came to be known as the Irish Literary Revival circumferenced my poetical life. Thereafter, that vision and enthusiasm became its centre, and circumferences learned not to matter. I ceased to be a citizen of my particular world—though that world had its own exquisite completeness—and was driven by the winds of destiny on the spiritual adventure of becoming, as fully as possible, a world polarized and orbited in a citizen.[15]

Cousins' interest in the Orient was not unique among other Irish writers of the time, the most notable in this regard being that of George Russell and William Butler Yeats. Russell had immersed himself in religious and spiritual works from the East, the name of his poetic personality—AE—being drawn from the symbol of the Hindu mantra for the sound of the ultimate universal reality, *om.* Yeats' fascination with the stylized dance dramas of Japan, the Noh plays, became, for him, a helpful influence on the dramatic expression of his developing beliefs in his mature years. But Yeats and Russell, along with their Irish contemporaries, derived their Eastern interests from afar, or from imported Eastern *gurus*. Cousins, distinctively, made real his interest. His attention to the East brought him there physically and spiritually, testifying to his strong belief in the reality of his spiritual convictions. It could be said that Russell and Yeats, in the Romantic tradition, longed for, or said they longed for, an immersion in an Eastern religious and artistic pattern of thought and action; but Cousins, singularly, acted. He abandoned

the security of his past to respond to his spiritual urging. This will to
make real his spiritual vision and beliefs underlies the writings and
works of his India years.

India, specifically the Theosophical Headquarters near Madras,
became the Cousins' home, or home base, for the rest of their lives,
a bit over forty years for James and some thirty-eight years for Gretta. For her, the years entailed continued involvement in women's
causes, her activities again leading her to a jail term. For Cousins,
the years entailed educational, cultural, and artistic activities,
basically growing from his Theosophical commitment.

He continued to write somewhat prolifically in a broad spectrum,
his works including poetry, drama, criticism, and Theosophical ex-
egesis. His growing notability as a writer and critic also took him
from India on a variety of foreign posts and lecture tours. For the
Cousins, the years were active and fulfilling; through them, both
James and Gretta retained and were informed by their vital spiritual
optimism and strong Theosophical outlook.

VI *Educational and Cultural Activities*

When the Cousins' arrived in India from Liverpool on November
1, 1915, Cousins took up his job as a literary editor of *New India*, a
paper published at the Theosophical Headquarters near Madras. A
year later, he began to teach—as he had in Dublin—but this time as
an English teacher at the Theosophical College in Madanapalle. He
became Vice-Principal of the school the following year, and in 1918
he was named its Principal.

He held a variety of educational positions in India in the decades
that followed. In 1922, leaving his Theosophical College Principalship when the college was closed, Cousins accepted the Direc-
torship of the newly-formed Brahmavidya Ashrama—School of
Universal Studies—which he had been instrumental in founding.
For Theosophical Society members, the school served to increase
their knowledge to aid in their interpretation of it "according to the
principles involved in the Three Objects of the Society: human
kinship unprejudiced by natural distinction; mutually helpful interest in all approaches to life; development of the latent powers of
the individual under the control and in the service of objects one
and two" (393). With Mrs. Besant's desire for a new school, and
Cousins' own interest in the synthetical study of the underlying uni-

ty of all matter and being, the primary ideas for the school had
come to Cousins in an informing and inspiring flash of awareness.
"One morning . . . I found myself looking at an imaginary sheet of
paper that had horizontal and parallel lines on it. I knew that I was
to fill it with suitable studies of the five main divisions of human activity: mysticism, religion, philosophy, art, science; and to study
them under five main aspects that nature has imposed on humanity:
substance, form, vitality, consciousness, superconsciousness. This
was, I was aware, the curriculum of the future school" (391).
Cousins remained Director until the spring of 1923. His continuing
interest in the school brought him in contact with a variety of people, especially Indians, interested in a wide range of cultural and artistic pursuits. Ideas generated by this experience underlie his
writings composed during that period and later.

Cousins reentered education once more, from 1933 - 1938, as
Principal of Besant Theosophical College in Madanapalle. In 1938
he became the Art Advisor to the Government of Travancore.

From his arrival in 1915, Cousins fostered and immersed himself
in numerous artistic and cultural ventures in India. His early years
there generated "enthusiasm for the arts and crafts of India and for
as much of its literature as I could absorb from English translations.
The aspiration and metaphysical imagination that radiated through
all these were sustenance and stimulus to my own" (397 - 98).
Because Cousins felt that Indians were provincially ignorant of the
work in art throughout India, he set out in 1923 "on a tour of
research into the cultural conditions of as much of India as I could
cover in a limited time, and into the possibility of founding centres
for the encouragement of local art—activities which might become
the eyes and ears and mouths of what I had begun to think of as a
central organisation fulfilling the needed purpose of record and ex-
change, and perhaps becoming the means of recognition of artistic
and literary 'immortals' after the manner of Academies elsewhere"
(398). He lectured on education and Indian art on the tour, which
took him from Madras through Calcutta, Benares, Agra, Delhi,
Amritzar, Srinigar, Hyderabad, Karachi, Ahmedabad, and Bombay.
In 1924, a collection of modern Indian paintings gathered by
Cousins was exhibited in the Jagan Mohan Palace in Mysore.

Cousins' continuing interest in art led to his appointment in 1934
as part-time advisor on art to the Travancore government, a position
he held for fourteen years. For two of those years, 1938 and 1939,

the position was full-time. Early in his tenure there, Cousins opened the State Art Gallery, and over the years he received a number of awards for his dedicated service and notable achievements. Then, in 1949, Cousins was named Vice-President of the Adyar Academy of the Arts—the Kalakshetra—at the Theosophical Headquarters. The Kalakshetra included a publishing company, a school, and a variety of social services. Cousins served there for the last seven years of his life.

VII *Travel*

Over the forty years that India was his home, Cousins travelled several times on journeys, some long in time and distance, from India. The year from April, 1919 to April, 1920, Cousins spent as a Guest Professor of Modern English Poetry in Keio University, Tokyo, traveling there by ship via Singapore, Hong Kong, and Shanghai. In Japan, Cousins went to Nikko, Atami, and Kyoto, and sought out Japanese paintings, some of which he said were "soulless" and "lacked idealism; and idealism was in my aesthetic credo, the test of the quality and life expectancy of any work of art" (353). Cousins also was depressed by what was for him the disease of modernism he found developing full-blast in sections of Tokyo. At the University, Cousins gave seven public lectures on Modern English Poetry, which he later published as a book, *Modern English Poetry*, in 1921.

By his own claim, Cousins became something of a "literary lion" in Japan. After his return to India, Cousins published in 1923 his *The New Japan: Impressions and Reflections*, to gratify friends who, he said, insisted that his experiences in Japan be put into book form.

Of the eight years from 1925 to 1933, Cousins spent almost five away from India, lecturing and travelling widely. In these years, he and Margaret undertook three major trips to Europe, with two of the trips continuing on to America and one stretching around the world for the return to India through the Orient. The first trip, from March to August, 1925, brought the couple through Italy and France to England and Ireland. In England, they renewed acquaintances with leaders of the women's movement. The visit to Ireland understandably stirred their emotions deeply. In the ten years since their departure, Ireland had been torn by revolution and fierce civil

strife. Age and separation had somewhat diminished their recollec-
tions of friends, and they noticed that the bonds of friendship
within the groups they remembered warmly had shifted. Political
and literary events had caused all to reconsider their alliances.

The Cousins' also recognized that they were disappointed in
many of the people who had once fascinated or intrigued them,
people whom they had once felt possessed the potential of
greatness. Yeats' presentation of himself, for example, with a long
lock of hair, dressed in a velvet jacket and wearing glasses on a long
tape, simply amused Cousins. When they spent an evening at Yeats'
home with George Russell, Oliver St. John Gogarty and Lennox
Robinson, the Cousins' were surprised at the "poverty of the conversation." They had expected much more of such a literary group
of eminent talkers. Subsequently an evening at the home of George
Russell, which they had greatly anticipated, turned into a disap-
pointment. The group of interesting Russell devotees, once so
stimulating, had dwindled to a single member—Padraic Colum.
Thus this evening too failed to meet their expectations. So too did
visits with Maud Gonne and Eamon DeValera.

Not all of Ireland seemed less splendid. After Dublin the Cousins
enjoyed a pleasant visit with Gretta's family and then went on to
Sligo where the natural beauty of Rosses Point and Ben Bulben had
not faded. Moreoever, Cousins was delighted with the newly won
freedom, the fruits of the revolution he had barely missed. His joy
in being surrounded by the natural beauty of an Ireland now free
moved him to write a twelve-line poem which George Russell
published in his agricultural and cooperative weekly.

During this 1925 trip, Cousins saw Synge's play, "The Playboy of
the Western World," produced in Liverpool by some Irish players;
and O'Casey's "Juno and the Paycock" in the Abbey Theatre. He
despaired of Synge's "back-street character" and expression and
lamented what he saw as a symbol of the decline of Irish theater.
"After a heart-breaking half-hour of vulgarity, I came out and shed
tears over the grave of dramatic idealism in the beginning of which
I had a share" (441). Cousins was of course not alone in this judgment but history has proven the judgment wrong. The characters
and the realism in the O'Casey play were not to Cousins' tastes,
either, and he concluded from that work too that the elevating tenor
of the theater had not developed as he had hoped—had in fact gone
off in a direction describable only as vulgar. "One could not judge

the real effect of the horrid story on the audience, for the ill-manners of the cheaper parts made judgement impossible. I was told that the post-freedom crowd had brought the theatre back to the early days of the dramatic revival, when the back streets had to be educated to look on a play as a serious work of art" (444).

The Cousins' world tour, beginning in April, 1928, was to spread "knowledge of Indian culture and life as we had found them" (445). The European travel included France, Belgium, Holland, Switzerland, England, and Ireland, where an evening was again spent with George Russell. In the United States, Cousins lectured in New York, Boston, Chicago, Iowa City, and Santa Barbara, and toured Hollywood and the Grand Canyon. The trip back to India included stops at Hawaii, Japan, and China.

Cousins travelled to Europe and America again in 1930. He left India in April alone, to be joined later by Gretta in New York City in July of 1931. Cousins lectured widely throughout the United States, on India, literature, and Theosophy. During 1931 - 32, his self-named "Skyscraper Year," he lectured at the City College of New York and worked with Gretta to found the New York Vegetarian Society, an endeavor of which they were always thereafter proud. Gretta attended courses in Teacher's College, Columbia University. They left New York in July, 1932. Gretta went on to India and James stayed on at the island of Capri for nine months before returning to India.

The time on Capri was an idyllic and productive one for Cousins. His dramatic impulse returned, along with a rekindled interest in Irish mythology, especially the Ulster cycle of Cuchulain, and the particular story of Cuchulain finding and releasing the exiled sons of Doel Dermait. In what he called a "visionary drama," Cousins "saw," while resting on a garden seat during a walk, the play he was being called to write. His writing of a somewhat long poem of one hundred and eight lines—"Bricriu's Feast," about the legendary Finn Mac Cool being diverted from duty by desire—gave Cousins the renewed courage to write his play, *The Exile of the Sons of Doel Dermait*. In March of 1933 he left Capri to accept the Principalship of Madanapalle College in India.

Neither Gretta nor James travelled again to the Western world. With the exception of a two-month trip to Java, Indonesia, and Bali in 1937—for a "first hand idea of the influence of Indian culture in the Far East"—the Cousins were to remain immersed in their many interests and activities in India (654).

VIII   *Enters Hindu Worship*

For Cousins, one of the most important symbolic acts of his religious life in his years in India was becoming a Hindu, in 1937. At the beginning of the ceremony marking his entering the religion, Cousins, "keenly aware of the historical significance and worldwide importance of the event," made a statement clarifying the meaning of his decision. The statement charted his religious development and beliefs. Cousins recalled it in this way in his autobiography:

I had been, I said, born into the Wesleyan Methodist sect of Christianity. My naturally reflective mind became dissatisfied with the religious exclusiveness of my upbringing. Modern science cut me away from all dogma; but an inborn religious sense and a truth-seeking mind would not allow me to rest in negation. I studied psychical research as it related to the dogma of immortality and the states of heaven and hell. I studied theosophy, and found in the Three Objects of the Society what appeared to me to be the fullest and most consistent method of approach to realisation of the truth of life. I studied books on the Vedanta, got to know certain of the Upanishads, memorised much of the Bhagavad Gita, and practised some phases of yoga. When I came to India I came to know of the cosmic and human symbolism of the deific figures and Pauranic stories, especially as embodied in sculpture and painting; also of the psychic influences that were gathered round and expressed in consecrated places and images. From these extensions of knowledge and experience I derived a deeper understanding of the universals of Christianity, though my return was at a level on which no believer in its historicity and universal obligation could meet me. I said these things in order to make it clear that my public declaration of belief in Hinduism as a way to union with the Divine Life, the way most in affinity with the devotee, the artist, and the philosopher in me, did not imply any denial of the spiritual truth that was to be found in all religions, or any repudiation of their ceremonial and discipline. To me the commonly used term conversion did not mean a turning away from one religion to another: it had for me the meaning of turning from the externals of any religion towards its internal and eternal verity. (644 - 45)

Cousins' flight from the narrowness of his religious training in Belfast and his belief that no one creed could contain the whole of truth brought him to this broad religious view, and his becoming a Hindu testified to his belief.

IX   *Gretta's Activities*

Gretta Cousins continued and strengthened her activities in promoting equality of rights for women in her years in India. From the time of her arrival in 1915, she was "revolted by the slavery and indignity put on womanhood by the inconsiderate domination of men, and there grew within me a determination to do all I could to forward all circumstances calculated to bring women into public and particularly legislative life, so that this evil and others might be rectified." She was especially shocked by "the forcing of motherhood on little girls, with its obvious evil influences on national physique, and its frustration of the mental development of its victims" (331).

She worked actively to promote her cause by continued lecturing and writing, notably a book, *The Awakening of Asian Womanhood* (Madras, 1922). She was a founding member in 1917 of the Women's Indian Association, and she initiated in 1931 the first All-Asia Women's Conference. Much of her energy went into social service, particularly for women and children.

In the course of her activities, she also was arrested in 1932 and jailed for one year for speaking against the English Ordinance Bill for India, which she, along with Gandhi and his followers, felt would seriously curb Indian rights to free speech and assembly.

X   *Cousins' Writings in India*

While James Cousins was active in the educational and cultural life of India, his Muse was never far away. As Cousins said, "I have tried in my time to be a reformer. But I don't know how. Poetry was always (but not quite always) breaking in" (698). His writing is in a broad range and is substantial. In the years from his arrival in India in 1915, Cousins published sixteen volumes of verse, two plays, seventeen books of criticism on literature or art, eleven volumes on educational, Theosophical, or cultural subjects, and over two dozen leaflets on various topics. Of singular mention, too, is *We Two Together*, a dual biography composed by James and Gretta during these years and published in 1950.

Cousins' idealism and his passion to reform the world, along with his muse, motivated most, if not all of this writing. As he himself pointed out, and as his verse verifies, nature was often a strong incitement to his verse-writing. No doubt, too, he found stimulus in the creative people he met, most notably the major Indian poet Rabindranath Tagore. Cousins had become interested in the writings of Tagore when he was introduced to them by Yeats in 1912. Soon after Cousins arrived in India, he met Tagore, and the two remained friends and acquaintances for several years. Tagore was helpful to Cousins in introducing him to cultural circles in India, and was a stimulus to his poetical endeavors. Cousins' volume of verse, *Surya Gita: Sun Songs,* was written for Tagore.

XI *Declining Years*

Gretta's health was the first to decline. In September of 1941, she collapsed while attending an All-India Educational Conference at Srinigar. While partially recovering, her health continued to fail, and in 1943 high blood pressure caused a stroke, which left her with some infirmities, including a paralyzed right hand. The following year she fell, fracturing a hip. She died at seventy-six years of age on March 11, 1954, with Cousins at her side. Cousins died about two years later, on February 20, 1956. In the last months of his life, he had had two serious falls, the second of which was two days before his death. James was eighty-two at his death. Both James' and Gretta's bodies were cremated.

Both had faced death with the firm foundation of their Theosophical outlook and anticipated an afterlife. "For ourselves, we have long anticipated the realities by looking for light in darkness and for ends in beginnings. We know for certain, not in the secondary sense of communication on information, but in the primary sense of experience observed and tested, that the human consciousness can function beyond its instruments of expression and impartation on the mundane plane, and beyond the phase of life called death; and we face the future with a realization of the discrepancies of our own relationship with reality that cannot be content to remain so, but that stretches its hand towards life after life for its completion" (770).

CHAPTER 2

Theosophical Thought and Prose Works

C OUSINS' lifetime drive away from narrowness, especially the
religious narrowness of his upbringing in Belfast, fostered his
attraction to Theosophy, a sect developing at the time. The
Theosophical Society was founded in 1875 by the Russian-born
Helena Blavatsky, and an American, Henry S. Olcott, who wanted
the Society to free the public mind from "theological superstition"
and to "tame subservience to the arrogance of science." The Society
saw itself as opposed to the dogmatism of organized religion and the
materialism of science. After its founding in New York City, units of
the Society appeared in major cities in Europe, including London
and Dublin. The world headquarters was established by Madame
Blavatsky in Adyar, Madras, India, largely because of the Society's
closeness to the Buddhistic and Brahmanic teachings of the East.

Madame Blavatsky was succeeded as head of the Society by Annie Besant in 1907, and the following year Mrs. Besant encouraged
the re-formation of the Dublin Theosophical Society. There had
previously been a shortlived unit in Dublin which had splintered
and dissolved in argument. Theosophy, while an unconventional
religion in Ireland, attracted and influenced a number of significant
writers and thinkers in Ireland in the years of the Celtic
Renaissance. Its basic principles appealed to Yeats and, more
strongly, to George Russell and Cousins, who was Russell's admirer
and associate. For Cousins especially, Theosophical thought became
the lifelong foundation for his identity and for his writing.

I *Theosophical Thought*

Theosophy—the term means knowledge of God—has as its basic
concept the postulation that there is a single benevolent source of
36

all creation, a First Great Cause, an Infinite Reality from which has come all tangible and intangible reality. This original spiritual essence is inherent in all things, in all matter, in all living things, in all humans, and in the very air that surrounds us. Everything is a manifestation of this single benevolent source; as a result, everything is basically united. From this postulation, Theosophy develops further an evolutionary pattern. Simply put—evolution begins at the perfect unity of the divine source, passes to a stage of fragmentation of perfection in earthly and tangible reality, and then moves toward, or, in fact, back to the point of, perfect unity, the point of beginning from which all things have come.

There is, then, matter with spirit inherent in it. Between matter and spirit springs up a polar relationship of opposites which tend always to reunite. As that reunion takes place, it gives rise to the phenomenon we call consciousness, itself another partial expression of the Universal Reality. In the evolutionary pattern, all that has descended and fragmented into material manifestation from the divine source is moving to ascend to the spiritual unity of that source. Everything, then, is essentially spirit, moving toward spiritual union. The essential spiritual unity of all things is the basis for the vegetarianism of Cousins and of many Theosophists, somewhat in the manner of George Bernard Shaw's saying he hadn't "eaten a fellow creature in years." Also, it is the basis for the strong belief in sexual equality and the rights of women, which led numerous Theosophists, male and female, including both James and Gretta Cousins, to be active in the suffragette movement in Ireland and in England early in this century.

A number of other principles appealing to Cousins follows from the belief in a divine First Cause and the consequent evolutionary pattern. Basic, of course, is that man is a god in the making and that there is not only evolution of soul, but also continuity of consciousness beyond death. Death is not annihilation. The possibility therefore exists of physical relationships beyond death, with communication with the Astral World made by mediums, by automatic writing, clairvoyance, or clairaudience.

Theosophical writers have written numerous studies developing and refining the operations of the immanence of God, the continuity of consciousness, the mechanism of consciousness, the evolution of soul, and the superphysical evolution. They have also written on the appeal and the satisfaction that they find in the principles of Theosophy. A central concept is that Theosophy is a religion and a science. One Theosophist has written that "We need a philosophy of life that is as scientific as it is beautiful, as logical as it is reverent. We need not only science of the material but a science of things spiritual . . . a science of the soul that satisfies the heart while it proves to the intellect that man is the deathless son of God, and that by right divine he walks the upward way of eternal life."[1] Theosophy, then, is looked on by Theosophists as a science dealing with tangible facts and the phenomena of the material scientist, and as a philosophy of life dealing with man, his origin, his evolution, and his destiny. It is also looked on as a religion, but in a lesser way, since Theosophy doesn't have a set of dogmas and a church that propagates them. Theosophists hold that all religions are of equal importance, an idea of special significance to Cousins, and that Theosophy provides a universal synthesis.

In 1913, Cousins published his small book, *The Bases of Theosophy*, in which he traced the founding of the Theosophical Society in New York, and outlined the two-fold purpose of the organization as "elucidation of fundamental and universal truth which lies at the root of all religion, philosophy and science," and the "cultivation of the fullest powers of humanity."[2] He clarified the central Theosophical belief of "the passing of the Unmanifest into manifestation, of the Absolute into the relative, of Unity into diversity, of Divinity into humanity."[3] As a result, then, "not only are we the children of a Divine Parentage: we are also the parents of a Divine Progeny."[4] In India, where Cousins felt religion was the instinctive mode of thought, he found the acceptance of "the principle of the One Absolute as source and goal of evolution"[5] as a sound basis for development in building an enlightened, cultivated, human society. He preferred, too, the dual sexuality of the deity in the East to the male deity in the West.

II   *The Appeal of Theosophy to Cousins and*
Other Irish Writers

Not surprisingly, Theosophy influenced particularly the idealistically political thought of the increasingly nationalistic writers in Ireland in the early decades of the twentieth century. A significant work in this regard is the important 1916 treatise, *The National Being*, by Cousins' friend George Russell. Cousins would no doubt agree with the Theosophical thinking that provided the basis for Russell's hope not only for the spiritual identity of Ireland as a country with its own national soul as a base for its existence as a nation separate from England, but also as a radiating influence for uniting all nations in harmony and love.

> I believe profoundly [wrote Russell], that men do not hold the ideas of liberty or solidarity, which have moved them so powerfully, merely as phantasies which are pleasant to the soul or make ease for the body; but because, whether they struggle passionately for liberty or to achieve a solidarity, in working for these two ideals, which seem in conflict, they are divinely supported, in unison with divine nature, and energies as real as those the scientist studies—as electricity, as magnetism, heat or light—do descend into the soul and reinforce it with elemental energy. . . . The amalgamation of individuals into nationalities and empires is as much in the cosmic plan as the development of highly organized beings out of unicellular organisms. I believe this process will continue until humanity itself is so psychically knit together that, as a being, it will manifest some form of cosmic consciousness in which the individual will share. . . . All these ideals of freedom, of brotherhood, of power of justice, of beauty, which have been at one time or another the fundamental idea in civilizations, are heavenborn, and descended from the divine world.[6]

But Theosophy appealed to Cousins and other writers for other than political reasons as well. Theosophy provided a comfortable assurance of a harmonious and benevolent union of the spiritual realm with the material, earthly realm at a time when science had brought scriptural assurances into question. Such a union had been a strong desire of major Romantic poets since Wordsworth—to see a benevolent infinite infused in the finite, although some Romantic poets—notably Byron and the later Coleridge—came to forsake or despair of such a single, benevolent, universal axis. Later, many Victorians came to suspect or lament the lack of such a union of the real and the ideal and expressed their loss in the thematic repetition of the lament of the withdrawal of God. Then, too, the implications of Darwin's thought and geological investigations had made suspect the divinity of man's creation. Theosophy, with its basic postulation of First Cause, obviated all the problems: there *was* benevolent divine immanence, since all things began and have evolved from perfect unity, have passed to a stage of fragmentation of perfection in earthly reality, and are evolving back to the point of perfect unity.

Theosophy also appealed to the Irish temperament. Perhaps one of the distinguishing characteristics of Anglo-Irish literature is its

persistently dual perspective, combining a perception of tangible
reality and a perception of intangible reality. This dual perception
results, very likely, from two sources: first, a vital primitive imagination preserved through geographical and historical causes; and
secondly, Ireland's actual confrontation with the realities of the
modern, and real, world.

Theosophy, by its very nature, appeals to this Irish dual perspective. Theosophy claims to bring into union the two realms.
Theosophists hold that Theosophy is a religion *and* a science, that it
satisfies the soul and the intellect; that it is a science dealing with
tangible facts and a philosophy of life dealing with man's origin,
evolution, and universal destiny. The combination of soul and intellect, of intangible and tangible that is at the base of Theosophical
principles by its very nature appeals to the range of perspective of
Cousins and other Irish writers of his period. This range of perspective also provides a foundation for the special relationships that
often exist literarily between Ireland and the East, between Ireland
and the Orient, as seen in Yeats' interest in the Noh plays of Japan.
The interfusion of the real and the spiritual that is significant in the
major religions of the East which echoes in the Irish perspective is
objectified by Theosophy. When Madame Blavatsky established the
Theosophical World Headquarters in India, she cited in her major
work, *The Secret Doctrine*, the East-West link it provided:
"Theosophy embraces much of the finest teachings of the world's
great religions. It combines the wisdom of the east with the logic of
the west and it weaves these into a living philosophy that offers
spiritual illumination and intellectual satisfaction."

George Russell's friend Monk Gibbon suggested also that
Theosophy provided Irish writers what the classics and classical
training had provided for other writers: it stood for a background of
culture, hard work, and mental discipline. Gibbon said that George
Russell "read the sacred texts [of Theosophy] as another man would
study Aristotle."[7] In this regard, the typical zeal and dedication of
Cousins no doubt stimulated his enthusiasm for reading Madame
Blavatsky.

Theosophy also appealed to Cousins and others who were
resisting the growing materialism in Ireland and the encroachments
of the middle class values—the values which were so clearly
abhorrent to Yeats and Cousins. The changing economic and com-
mercial life of Ireland made more attractive the spiritual values that
Theosophy preached, values more akin to traditional Irish values

than to those of a modern economic system. George Russell called attention to the threat of these economic encroachments:

We have always tried to steer by the stars, to endeavour to make our readers remember . . . that in the midst of all these immediate matters, these needs of the week or the day, humanity, a strange cavalcade, was journeying on to divine events and awful and august climaxes and judgments. It is not the business of an economic journal to preach these things; but it is, all the same, an urgent duty laid on us not to forget them, or in what fields we will camp when our journey is over . . . The fashion of the days is to keep the needs of the body in watertight compartments, and it is a fashion we hate.[8]

Theosophy also provided Cousins and others an escaping and enlarging idea of self in contrast with the narrowness and the provincialism of Ireland in this period. This has specifically religious implications in the case of Cousins, in flight from his Belfast Protestant background. Theosophy provided a world devoid of universal evil, in which there was a validity of self in time and matter and in which there was the assurance of the continuation of one's spirit in an alluring spiritual perfection.

III   *Theosophy and Mythology*

Of particular interest is the appeal of Theosophy in providing a way of reading and interpreting the newly important Celtic mythology so central to writers of the Irish Literary Movement. Cousins states this directly:

The personalities and events of the Irish mythos became to me the imaginative incarnations of powers and processes in the universe and myself. I felt that vision was more ultimate than insight and more prophetic than foresight; and through its contemplation and embodiment in my early poems I aspired toward the capacity to see the significance of the insignificant and to feel the eternal in the temporal.[9]

To be drawn to the "other-world" of mythology was a common dedication of Cousins and other poets and prose writers in Ireland at this time. For verse writers, mythological material provided inspiration for creating imagined perfect realms, for romantically primitive, unspoiled kingdoms and modes of being. The nineteenth-century interests in philology and in pursuit of defining "national soul" had motivated discovery of and interest in ancient Irish myths and manuscripts throughout the libraries of Europe and revealed to Ireland what Cousins called a literature "epic in grasp; lyric in impulse; full of feeling after colour, and music and form; subtle, naive, simple, barbarically splendid."[10] Cousins' interpretative study of Irish mythology, *The Wisdom of the West*, is an important work not only in clarifying his thinking on mythology and Theosophy, but also in suggesting the importance of Theosophy to all literature, and to Cousins' own writing. Like other Irish authors, Cousins sought spiritual identification with the older Celtic spirit submerged by the conqueror. This identification was for him at once philosophic, religious, and realistic. He felt strongly that myth had a meaning in fact, provided one recognized that any given moment in one's life immediately passes and becomes "a matter of history"; "one's life of a year ago has passed into the realm of the mythological." Thus, one's own life is continually merging with the past, and one's being, though continuing in the present, simultaneously becomes one with all that has preceded it. As such, Irish mythology "is as much to be reckoned with, as a fact of life, as the practical man's struggle with a crochety balance-sheet." (5 - 6)

At the same time myth became for Cousins as it did for Thoreau, "the most ancient history and biography," containing essential and enduring truth; the myth is a story with eternal reality in it. "The myths of our forefathers contained *in potentia* the most advanced thought of today as . . . the flower is contained in the seed from which it sprang." And by extension of this concept of myth, Cousins concluded that in the final analysis, myth is a kind of "Word made flesh" (15 - 18), and is filled with moral lessons. The symbols in myth of "fabulous power, fabulous chivalry, fabulous swiftness, fabulous beauty" touch the reader to reach out to his own "superlative endowments" (6 - 7). In this, Cousins adopts a point of view similar to that of Shelley, claiming that simple moral codes or rules are ineffective teachers, but that the beauty and content of Irish mythology provide an effectively uplifting and ultimately good moral code: "The moral and ethical import is of immense service . . . to patriotism and humanitarianism" (8). While this view of myth seems to omit the crimes recorded in Celtic mythology, Cousins found in it an endorsement of his own optimistic religious and philosophical thought.

He did not consider this an airy escapism: it represented his solution of the Victorian problem of the conflict of faith and nature. His maturing years in Belfast had brought him to read Arnold, Huxley, and Darwin. In Celtic myth, Cousins found what he said mythology presented, a basic theory of life.[11] The high quality of Celtic mythology, he thought, implied and probably expressed the high level of civilization of the ancients; it was therefore a mistake to conclude on the basis of evolutionary theory that myth was a product of ancestral savages. Indeed, far from barbarism, myth was the "unfailing refuge of the consciousness which has exhausted the possibilities of the world of intellect."[12] Also, in Celtic mythology (unlike the Greek), he saw a theory of existence far different from the evolutionary one of constant development from a rudimentary primordial organism to an ultimate evolved perfection. Celtic mythology, he believed, also showed an outlook far different from the dualistic one of the Hebraic-Christian tradition, in which God, the principle of good, and Satan, the principle of evil, are separate forces distinctly apart. Celtic theology seemed to him to be monistic, and to confirm his belief that the universe emanated from one unknowable principle which lies behind, permeates, and unifies all. As this perfect principle manifested itself, it developed many personifications, frequently in balanced opposing groups, with each group having basic goodness in it since each had developed from the single initial unknowable force. Just as is understood in terms of modern physics, the polarity inherent within the overall force itself caused each element to be essentially formed by two diametrically opposed forces. Yet the complementary quality of the poles resulted in overall harmony, and each element has a significance of its own which is merely augmented by association with other elements.

As Celtic mythology presents this outlook in its stories, marriages transmit and transform the idea of duality, the proper marriage being the uniting of two good opposites. This unification reflects a return to the original, single, unknowable creative force of being, a fulfillment of foreordained reunion. In this view, all things began in a state of oneness at the seat of perfection and have evolved into many forms, including the earthly, bodily, or concrete realm, which contain in themselves the seeds of the divine. Hence, in the myths, the individual man and woman when joined together, stand as a microcosm of Godhead. There is moreover the assumption that the earthly realm will in its continuing evolution, through similar uniting of the spiritual essences within its elements, return to the total unified essence of the initial creative entity.

Cousins develops his view of the Celtic philosophy behind the myths in this fashion:

The first principle of the Cosmos is an unknown and unknowable unity, which passes into the duality which runs through all manifest things, as positive and negative, spirit and matter, masculine and feminine, Formorians and De Danaans, Dagda and Dana. But these dualities cannot be regarded as absolute entities; the existence of the other, and their interaction is manifested as a trinity consisting first of essential being; secondly, of power and will, which is the attribute of the Cosmic Mind; thirdly, of activity, which is the essence of manifestation. From these spring life, which presses into multiplicity; each atom being a partaker of the essential being, a sharer in the Cosmic will, an exponent of the universal activity, an epitome of the whole. The Divine Substance passes from degree to degree until, as we inadequately say, in human speech, it loses all semblance of Divinity: Dana, the universal mother, as her name implies, *dwindles*, as the primal impulse sweeps down to its ordained limit. Then comes a change. Dana reappears as Brigit the *expander;* consciousness is evoked, and grows and grows, and cannot cease growing until it becomes one with the Universal Consciousness. (50 - 51)

Simply, evolution begins at perfect unity, passes to a stage of fragmentation of perfection in earth and reality, and eventually ends back at the point of beginning, at perfect unity. It is on this basis that Cousins dismissed his early concepts of heaven and hell, the saved and the damned: for Christianity allows no such reconciliation or unification of the force of evil, personified in Satan, and the force of good, personified in God or Christ. It is also on the basis of this revelation in mythology that Cousins resolved the vertical evolutionary theory drawn from nineteenth-century scientific and geological exploration.

But Greek myth was different from the Celtic and the Vedic mythologies of the East. Greek myths differed in that the gods were drawn very distinctively, in clearly defined symbolism, which possibly enhanced the myths' aesthetic value. Celtic and Vedic gods, Cousins felt, were not distinctively drawn, were not compartmentalized: everything bore a relationship to everything else, all atoms were interdependent. Celtic mythology was "sensitive, suggestive," while Greek mythology was "definite, unambiguous, solid" (28 - 29). Celtic mythology in its vagueness and with its pantheism allowed for a spiritual essence to pass through many forms, with rebirth and metempsychosis as common events; uniquely, in Celtic rebirth, the human consciousness was frequently retained.

Cousins concluded that the Greek conception of the origin of gods was a natural one; the Celtic conception of the origin of gods was supernatural or spiritual.

In Ireland, the arrival of Christianity and the Normans, Cousins thought, prevented Celtic thought from developing naturally. In the Celtic outlook, all emanations were from a divine source, and male and female were dual manifestations. The only possible Christian counterpart, an equal worship of a male Christ and a female Mary was both inferior of itself and absolutely prohibited. But the Christian bases themselves became particularly repellent to Cousins.

A religious system results which in so far as it relates to an arrogant and bloodthirsty Deity, is a gross libel, and in so far as it relates to a cringing and cowardly humanity is a flat insult to human intelligence. I confess a much greater sympathy with Oisin, who scorned Patric and his bell-ringing clerics, than with some nonentity who escapes the consequences of a life of sin by giving a hurried assent to the death of an innocent victim at the behest of an angry God. (34)

Cousins' flight from Wesleyan Methodism was a tenacious one.

Myth and Theosophy, then, were closely intertwined for Cousins, each providing support and interpretative enlargement for the other. The creators and developers of mythological stories were seen as knowing intuitively the history, the truth, the eternal realities of the relationship between the material and the supernatural worlds. The insights of the creators of the myths testified that ancient man, rather than having descended from apes or savages, had originated from the benevolent force that Theosophy posited. Irish myth, like the mythologies of India and the East, seemed similar in its insights into these eternal realities, and superior to the mythological insights of Greece and the West, which had become limited by reason and intellectual order.

IV   *Theosophy and War*

The first part of the century brought not only the growing political turmoil in Ireland's struggle for independence, including the bloodshed of the 1916 rebellion, but also the conflict that involved all of Europe in the Great War. Such struggles tested the optimism of Cousins' Theosophical beliefs. From whence came such horror and destruction in a world and universe progressing in the

Theosophical pattern presented in Cousins' reading of history and myth? His small volume, *War: A Theosophical View*, discusses his position; it places war in a universe of untiringly active and progressive good. Within the Absolute Unity that Theosophy posits, the opposites of energy and substance are actually in affinity. Energy, to manifest itself, needs substance to act upon, and substance needs energy acting upon it so that it becomes shaped and defined, so that it does not remain inchoate. Together, both energy and substance work for and move toward the return to ultimate unity. The process includes struggle, and war is part of that struggle. Substance wants fixity; energy wants to break form to shape or reform a better or higher order. With this Theosophical viewpoint applied to history, Cousins reads the destruction of Rome by the Germanic tribes as the dawn of a new era. "War," he holds, "is not a fatal opposition between contending forces, but a vital cooperation between affinities in the vast process of human evolution."[13] Cousins also approaches the Great War in this way, and musters his facts to support his view that the War is part of the unifying process. The map of Europe he saw was tangible evidence of the process. In the past, Europe had progressed from small tribal dukedoms to large nations. With the coming of World War I, Cousins noted that nations were linked in endeavor on both sides—nations which were previously at odds with one another. Also, for Cousins, the War had functioned to dissolve political, ideological, even economic separations within individual countries. Competing entities within England, for instance, were now united in facing the common danger. The dissolution of divisions within and between nations could not, said Cousins, be seen as "mere accidental goodnesses struck out of something essentially and entirely evil. They are signals to us that within the apparently evil there is a spring of good; that, indeed, if we have a sufficiently wide view of things, the good that is in evil is predominant, and will be seen in due time. Hard as it is to realize this now, with horror piled on horror in our newspapers, it is nevertheless true, and will be seen so when this gigantic discord is resolved by time to a gigantic harmony" (13 - 14). Cousins ventures that the better future "may see the complete emergence of the feminine regenerative influence" after the present struggle between "purely masculine powers," since "the avowed objective of the allies is the abolition of force as the final argument in human affairs, and the elevation of ideals of justice and mutuality that must apply to all phases of thought and action" (15).

In mentioning the dissolution of divisions within individual nations, Cousins suggests thinking similar to that of George Russell, evident in his later work, *The National Being*. The cosmic process operates "not only in the units of consciousness called human beings, but in the congeries of units called nations" (16). Hence, for Cousins as for Russell, nations have a national being, or national soul. For this, Cousins cited the law of Karma in Indian philosophy as his comparative source.

While Cousins expressed his sympathy for the deaths and the human suffering caused by the War, he put them, too, in an optimistic Theosophical perspective which, he held, provided an understanding of the suffering that helped in coping with it. Life, he claimed, being one and indestructible, cannot be taken away, cannot be killed. Death is merely a process of life and has no power over it. Life precedes birth and continues after death. Conscious human existence is an interval, "one episode in a long series of similar episodes—a series of experiments, so to speak, in physical science, for the purpose of expanding spiritual science" (24). Hence, for Cousins, those killed in war were not cut off in the prime of life but were merely propelled into the next stage more precipitously than others. Cousins found consolation also in the thought that "early death in discharge of an ennobling duty, and in circumstances of exalted emotion, is probably a much more valuable experience to the soul than a long life of dull commonplaceness" (26). Thus the tangible and widespread turmoil, pain, and death of the Great War became for Cousins a test against which he could examine the philosophical operations and consolations of Theosophy. The fact that he succeeded in rationalizing the war and that he could actually view the horrors of the trenches as a step forward in the spiritual and emotional journey of mankind toward perfection clearly demonstrates the consistency of Cousins' view. It might also suggest that the tenacity with which he clung to the tenets of Theosophy crippled his capacity to empathize with his fellow creatures and led to a narrowed perception of and diminished appreciation for that which he dismissed as tangible reality. It also sets him apart from the majority of contemporary writers who felt and explored the disillusionment brought by the intense suffering and widespread loss of life that the war more accurately represented.

V *Theosophy and Cousins' Educational Principles*

Cousins' years in teaching and in educational administrative posts lead to his careful amalgam of Theosophy and the aims of education.

Cousins' outstanding work in this regard is *A Study in Synthesis* (1934), which AE told him was a

remarkable and stimulating book, your very best work in prose . . . Your mind has never moved so clearly . . . I am glad to think of your intellect opening and widening in this way.[14]

The book was the culmination of Cousins' six years as founder and director of the Brahmavidya Ashrama (School of Universal Study) at Adyar, a

school for the synthetical study of universal knowledge and culture on the principle that these in their racial, religious, national, local and individual aspects, are essentially related and mutually illuminating expressions of one Cosmic life.[15]

Cousins' own studies for these years he collected in this volume, the aim of which he elaborated upon in his Preface:

Synthesis is primordial, essential, integral. It is not a condition to be attained; it is a fact of life to be realised and acted upon. A mere eclecticism (a mere piecing together of things, even of the best things) can never be vital. The bread of life comes out of no synthetical bakery. My "Study" therefore is not of an attainable synthesis through fitting things together; but of an inescapable synthesis of fundamental human capacities through which the life of the universe may be liberated into expression that will naturally become synthetically orderly instead of analytically chaotic as it is at present.[16]

The studies at the School of Universal Study were to arouse students "to their own inner synthesis as soon as possible."[17]

The book is a complex and detailed one with several series of diagrams illustrating the broad and the specific syntheses—the Creative Synthesis, including art, poetry, and words; the Contemplative Synthesis, including philosophy and beauty; the Observative Synthesis, including science, religion, and the future; the Associative Synthesis, including society and civilization; and the

Educational Synthesis, including the student as a feeler, thinker, and doer.

Within each synthesis, there are four subdivisions of kind: Intuition, Cognition, Emotion, and Action. Intuition includes inspiration and illumination; Cognition includes philosophy and science; Emotion includes religion and art; Action includes organization and execution. Hence, in the synthesis of the Arts we have as Intuitive, poetry and music; as Cognitive, *belles lettres*, fiction, and drama; as Emotive, song and dance; as Active, painting and sculpture. In the synthesis of Religion we have as Intuitive, Hinduism and Zoroastrianism; as Cognitive, Buddhism and Jainism; as Emotive, Christianity and Islam; as Active, Hebraism and Shinto. The Educational Synthesis follows this pattern with the study of lives of the seers and meditation in the Intuitive category; philosophy, pure science, and applied science in the Cognitive category; comparative religion, art study, and art work in the Emotive category; history, sociology, biology, and physical education in the Active category. All four categories should be developed and then united in the total unifying synthesis. The balance line in all of these areas is that separating the perfect from the actual: inspiration from realization, universal truth from local fact, devotion from observance. It is basically Cousins' refinement of his concern for the unification of the supernatural and the natural, the abstract and the actual, that is evident in his verse, which frequently attempts to rise to and beyond the "verge"—a word which recurs in Cousins—the borderline of the spirit realm.

Of especial interest is the subdivision for a Synthesis of Word. Here the basic separation is between the verb, defined as energy, and the noun, defined as substance.

In the interaction of the verb and noun, and their fulfilment in the sentence, we have the speech reflection of the cosmic law of the interaction of energy and substance, which the Hindu imagination embodied in the gods and their *shaktis* (goddesses) who cannot function apart from one another, and in the social convention of husband and wife being essential to perfect performance of the daily ceremonial of the Brahmin home. (171)

As parts of speech are developed and interpreted, common nouns "express the result of the union of energy and substance" (172); qualitative adjectives express "a unity of substance" while proper adjectives express "a unity of idea" (171). Other parts of speech are

similarly developed and interpreted. This analysis of words, then,
Cousins said, leads

on to grammar as the form-basis of speech; thence to the vital element in
words and literature; then to the conscious content and technique of verse
and prose; lastly to the super-conscious influences, particularly in
verse—illumination, inspiration, imagination, psychic incursion, that have
received little or no attention at the hands of students of literature. What
applied thus to verbal expression applied to all subjects. (469)

While not profound, *A Study in Synthesis* is a remarkable undertaking as it attempts to interpolate an order and direction on what
Cousins views as a fluid universe. In its own words, it is a cognitive
work approaching the problem of universal order from a purely
rational, intellectual point of view, imposing orderly structure on
the facets of human existence. And it is not unsophisticated in either
its psychology or formal philosophy. But it does suffer, as do so
many of Cousins' works, from a static quality born of his ego. The
most successful and stimulating and exciting philosophical theories
derive from a dynamic questioning and seeking. *A Study in
Synthesis* is, on the contrary, a dry exposition of what the author
already knows to be the truth, and it presents itself as beyond
challenge.

The pith of Cousins' educational philosophy and activities is implicit in the Educational Synthesis in *A Study in Synthesis*. It is
more generally stated in his volume, *The Kingdom of Youth*, in
which he defines a Trinity of education: "a free soul working
through a sound mind and a sound body."[18] Of significance here is
the "free soul," elsewhere in the book called the Imagination, "the
link between the individual and the universe" (18). Cousins held,
"there can be no true educational advancement so long as the place
of Imagination in life is unrealized, and the furnishing and development of Imagination is neglected" (29). A true education should be
available to both sexes and to all classes, including the "submerged
classes" of India, to produce a needed new birth in literature, the
arts, religion, and social organization. This outlook was the foundation of his various teachings and administrative positions in
Theosophical schools in India.

VI   *Theosophy and Cousins' Critical Writings*

The foundation for all of the critical assessments by Cousins was his own personal philosophy with its basis in Theosophical thought. Cousins approached and evaluated the wide range of cultural fields that interested him and the artistic efforts in each as they revealed awareness of an ideal spiritual realm and aided in moving human consciousness toward the ultimate spiritual unity of which he was assured. The arts, for him, were significant for their philosophical and spiritual relevance.

In his *The Faith of the Artist*, he traced the importance of the arts in his own life and stated his outlook on their central relevance. In his consciousness from boyhood had been the subject of "the nature of the art-impulse in myself and others, and its relationship to the individual and general life, the latter including the interaction of nations." As he matured, he came to a realization that creative art was "the only possible restorer of lost faith" (7), and that "the growing evil in . . . the arts in general in the world arose out of ignorance of the reality and spiritual purpose of the impulse to art-creation" which brought the

conviction that variety of independent experience of the influence behind the arts, and declaration of such experience, are essential to the proper placing of the arts among the forces of life. (15)

The experiences referred to were those of psychic inspiration.

In his *Work and Worship*, stating his belief that the spirit would, in the course of evolution, overtake and dominate the flesh, Cousins pointed out that for him, cultural activity was in reality "active participation in the process of creation,"[20] with each individual art "untrue, inasmuch as no part can express the whole."[21] The range of art was from earthly realism to spiritual realism, with spiritual realism having the greatest value because it revealed "the inner nature of things," for "when the magic wand invokes the Spirit which sits at the centre of life, it becomes true realism, for then it is face to face with the Reality on which all else hangs."[22]

Such spiritual realism Cousins saw in Bengal painting during his time in India, and more generally in much of Indian and Oriental art, a subject of some of his critical attention. Indian art, he wrote in *The Renaissance in India*, had escaped "the divorce between the arts and religion and philosophy"[23] that had afflicted European culture. While in Europe, "the predominant . . . activity is analysis, separation, specialisation, not merely in affairs of daily life, but in the things of the mental life,"[24] "in India . . . there has been no such separation made between the various functions of humanity."[25] Hence he saw the artist in India as an artist and a philosopher at the same time. For Cousins, the highly regarded artists were those who presented a spiritual vision that was indicative of the ultimate, unifying, spiritual reality. This spiritual vision was also, for Cousins, the foundation of an Eastern unity that he enlarged upon in his *Cultural Unity of Asia*, which traced the origins of the three kinds of Asian religions—Aryan, Semitic, and Mongolian—to a common source, vaguely called the "Primitive Asian Religions."[26] He saw India as the mother of Asian Culture, just as in Ireland he had seen Irish mythological primitives as providing a unified point of origin.

Cousins also sought out and praised spiritual realism in his critical statements on literature. While in Ireland, his values had developed strongly enough that he valued the poetic genre over the dramatic, though he was both a playwright and poet at the time. In articles in newspapers, *The United Irishman* and *The Pioneer*,[27] he pointed out that the playwright, using his powers of observation, held a mirror up to nature, transcribing a current scene for the audience, which received the scene with their senses. The poet, though, with the God-given gift of the seer, would hold nature itself up to the mirror and thereby present timeless truth to be absorbed by the very being, "the inner ear," of the listener.

In Ireland, Cousins shared Russell's vision of divine immanence—"the old spiritual monism of the mythmakers."[28] Cousins regarded highly the spiritual content of AE's poetry. Joseph Holloway, the contemporary inveterate theatergoer, records that "In Mr. Cousins' opinion Mr. George Russell is the 'Daddy of them all' in the Literary revival."[29] AE's work met the standard of what Cousins set out in his essay, "Mysticism in English Poetry," as the highest possible mystical poetic achievement: "The highest conception of a poetic entity is that in which the white light of central spirit burns through, illuminates and transfigures the successive planes, radiating through the ethical and moral to the outermost crust of the material, and transmuting the substance of each into the likeness of spirit, of which, indeed, they are but differentiations of intensity and vibration."[30]

But, while he greatly respected AE's work, Cousins insisted that "Mysticism may be expressed poetically; but is not necessarily therefore poetry." So that while AE's mysticism was of a superior nature, his poetry was not. Compared with the mystical poets Shelley and Blake, AE was "a mystic who writes poetry" and to

Cousins the difference was significant. For while AE's mystical vision was superior, his poetry was not as skillful as Shelley's. Russell's poetry had a "peculiar feature as of a preconcerted movement in one direction, as though its trees were bending always to westward before a wind which blows for ever from the East."[31] Russell was, for Cousins, "a greater *knower* than Shelley, but a lesser artist."[32]

Praise for Shelley recurs in Cousins' critical statements, with his fundamental outlook summarized in *The Renaissance in India*. Shelley's unwavering idealism presented in its lyric beauty was the primary attraction. "Every paragraph" of "Prometheus Unbound" is "pervaded by spiritual illumination; and there are stanzas in 'Adonais' (the forty-third for example) that might serve as headings for a lecture on Spiritual Solution. Yet with true art, the thought, emotion, architecture and expression of 'Prometheus Unbound' are so integral, so mutually interfused, that its appeal is all-compelling from whichever of the quaternary of qualities we regard it."[33] Cousins was admiring of poetic expression of the idea of reincarnation in "Adonais" and "Prometheus Unbound." In 1933, Cousins developed and refined his examination of Shelley in *The Work Promethean: Interpretations and Applications of Shelley's Poetry.*

The works of Shelley, followed in time by those of George Russell, were, for Cousins, philosophic milestones in evolution of the awareness of mankind, an evolution revealed in an "evolution of poetry" that "will move naturally from the outer to the inner, from sensation to the higher emotions, and thence to spiritual illumination and exaltation. That is the general tendency, and anything that comes from the higher degrees of poetical consciousness will call up the whole art of poetry towards its culmination."[34]

In *Footsteps of Freedom,* Cousins charts his evidence from literature of the developing human awareness. His aim was "to point out a few of the Footsteps of Freedom in English Literature, mainly in the poets, who are specially responsive to impressions from 'principalities and powers' beyond the horizon of the ordinary individual."[35] The authors selected include Dante, Edmund Burke, Wordsworth, Shelley, John Stuart Mill, Walt Whitman, the unknown Henry Bryan Binns, and "those Irish who kept the spirit of Irish verse alive for centuries." His later lectures in Tokyo, published in his *Modern English Poetry,* were based on the premise that modern English poetry had not caught up with Blake and Shelley as yet. The volume discusses Indian, American, English, and Irish verse contribution to a future for poetry and onward to the ultimate spiritual vision of fundamental unity. The Irish race is praised for "a consciousness of a larger life than that which is contacted by the five senses."[36]

In *New Ways in English Literature*, Cousins discusses along with lesser figures, Tagore, Yeats, and Synge. He objects to Synge's realism. Synge is seen as a mere copyist, a shaper and craftsman with no vision of unity in the divine. Yeats is valued for his use of myth and because his fairies "are no figures of speech . . . they are realities."[37] Tagore is praised by Cousins for giving body and emotion to the thought of the interaction of the relative and the absolute, for his combining of poetry and philosophy.

The evidence of Cousins' personal beliefs is apparent throughout all of his critical works, and they become his main measure of judgment. This is a serious critical limitation. The foundation that Cousins uses for all of his critical judgments is the tenuous, unproven and unprovable beliefs of Theosophy. He approaches every literary work with these preconceptions and accepts and finds value only in those which mesh with and fit into his world view. With these works which are acceptable to him, he then builds insubstantial support for the Theosophical assumptions with which he began, which are now, from his point of view, reinforced as the foundation for subsequent critical judgments. A self-assuring and self-assured cycle is thus made complete.

These Theosophical beliefs, nevertheless, provided the motivation for all of his activities in the literary, cultural, and educational endeavors; it was these beliefs that drew him from Ireland in a manner different from the removal from Ireland of Joyce and other Irish expatriates. Rather than rebel against Ireland, Cousins drew from it the beliefs he found through the Celtic myths, and he held fast to them. Ireland had produced him and he was always proud of his roots. Ireland, too, was always accommodating to him. His Theosophical idealism was comfortably appealing to his contemporary writers and, from the few short contemporary reviews of his works in Ireland, were sympathetically received by the public. Theosophy itself had seemingly found fertile ground in the imaginative idealism that marks this period in Ireland.

In discussing Cousins' Theosophical thinking and its intertwinement with his writing in educational philosophy and artistic and literary criticism, it would be amiss to neglect citing his extraordinary autobiography, *We Two Together*, written in conjunction with his wife, Gretta. This dual autobiography by Cousins is a revealing and not especially modest interleafed and detailed telling of the lives of each, focusing on their Theosophical pilgrimage as it shaped their thinking, their literary works, their activities and travel, and brought them honors and associations with notable people. The triple redundancy in the title, *We Two Together,* calls attention to the Cousins' belief in the equality and the uniting of the sexes and to the Cousins' spiritual union as part of the ongoing process of progressing toward a universal unity.

CHAPTER 3

The Plays

ALMOST all of Cousins' plays were written while he was
in Ireland, though he did produce some dramatic efforts in
India. An enthusiast of the early Celtic Renaissance, in Dublin he
was swept into acting and into attempting to provide the Irish plays
sought for at the time. His plays, which draw almost exclusively on
legends, myths, and stories of Irish life, reflect this, as do his concern for presentation of mood and his work in verse drama.

Cousins told of his early interest in writing plays in the preface to
his later verse play, *The Clansmen*. When he wrote his narrative
poem, "Ben Madighan," in Belfast in 1890, he wanted also to put
its Irish subject matter on stage—to write Irish drama. He resisted
the urge, though, because of the sentiment of those around him.
"Theatre," he knew, "was the mouth of hell to my good parents
and most of my friends."[1] When he later went to Dublin, met
George Russell and the Fay brothers, he was able to overcome the
effects of this scruple and his career in the drama developed.

The Clansmen, the play he first wrote in Belfast, he resurrected
and reworked in 1903 - 4. The encounter of Mac Gilmore and
Savage, a pagan and a Christian, is dramatized in four acts of
imitation-Shakespeare blank verse. The plot moves somewhat
spasmodically. The first act is given over to long exposition as two
friars, one a tedious comic who is counterfeit Shakespeare, discuss
the unblessed union of Hugh Mac Gilmore, a pagan, and Mary
Savage, a Christian. Act II opens with further exposition, now of a
Mac Gilmore - Savage battle in which Hugh Mac Gilmore has killed
the brother of his wife, Mary Savage. The scene itself then focuses
on the guilt Mac Gilmore feels, which prompts his revelation to his
wife that his father had slain her father. Even with such deepened
enmity, however, Mary Savage remains angelically loyal to her husband. It is made clear that she is goodness personified and is in her
pureness drawing his soul to freedom, thus fulfilling the prophecy
that one would come to lead the Mac Gilmores to Christianity. As
56

the act closes, one of the friars arrives and speaks first of God's mysterious ways and then of the slaying, in lines echoing *Macbeth:*

> Oh! cursed be the hand that wrought this deed.
> And cursed be the brain that gave it birth.[2]

The friar also refuses to help the ailing Mac Gilmore, an enemy, even though Mary pleads with him, reinforcing her plea with quoted Scripture.

Act III opens with the friar's change of heart; he decides to help the sick Mac Gilmore and explains his decision in lines in the style of Cousins' narrative verse:

> My daughter, there are times and seasons meet
> For giving, and for taking—when the light
> Of laughter and forgetfulness doth play
> Like summer sunbeams on a river's face,
> Obscuring mostly where they most illume—
> But when illusion's veil is rent in twain,
> As was the Temple's; when the holy place
> In soul and soul stands open and revealed;
> Then, need and satisfaction equal move
> To the one measure, breathing common breath:
> For in the silence at the heart of things
> There is no room for deeds that ask for thanks.[3]

This moment of awakening is spoken in some of the best lines of the play. They move with a calmly regular tone, speaking of the "one measure," the "common breath," the ultimate spiritual unity. Mary's purity has been a "goad to goodness," and the remainder of the play reveals that essence of goodness working through the characters and the action. Although Mary is accidentally shot by her brother, she dies contentedly as she goes to enlightenment:

> . . . I feel
> A breaking of the buds: a shining form
> Uplifts a foamy tankard full of Spring
> To flame-red lips, and moves beneath a sky
> Of apple blossoms.[4]

The last act brings a sobered and repentant Mac Gilmore to embrace the Church as he dies. Mary's brother, a Savage, remorsefully stabs himself over the Mac Gilmore corpse.

The play is not a success, and it never saw the stage. Dramatic action is not the focal point of the play, and the plot is not well-managed. The exposition is labored: the moral is too heavily pronounced. Although the play is very likely a fulfillment of the task he set himself and contains some good but isolated poetic lines in blank verse, Cousins is too slavishly devoted to Shakespeare. The attempt to impose his Theosophical philosophy on dramatic tragedy is a failure.

I   The Sleep of the King

A significant number of the playwrights of the Irish Renaissance, Synge being a notable exception, brought with them an impulse toward and a background in verse writing. Cousins' drama is influenced by his concern for mood, poetic imagery, and rhythmic utterance. In Dublin, he further brought to his dramatic composition his interest in Irish legend, specifically in his verse drama of mood, *The Sleep of the King*,[5] a presentation of the story of Connla of the Golden Hair from P. W. Joyce's *Old Celtic Romances*, suggested to Cousins by Frank Fay. Joyce had found the story, "Echtra Condla Cain," in the significant source, *The Book of the Dun Cow*, where "Oisin in Tir na nOg" was also found by Yeats. Both stories are tales of fairies taking mortals to more idyllic realms. The Connla story was transcribed into the Dun Cow volume about 1100 A.D., from an older manuscript. King Conn, father of Connla, was King of Ireland from A.D. 123 to 158. Joyce entitled the story, "Connla of the Golden Hair." His story tells of King Conn and his son Connla, standing on the royal hill of Usna on a day when a beautifully attired maiden appeared, seen only by Connla, but heard by both father and son. The maiden entreats Connla to join her in the Land of the Living, the "plain of never-ending pleasure" where he will retain "comeliness and dignity . . . free from the wrinkles of old age." Conn summons his Druid, who is able to force the maiden to retire, but as she goes she tosses a marvelous apple to Connla. Though he eats from it every day for a month and takes no other food, the apple never lessens and Connla remains sustained. After the month the maiden reappears from the West to entreat Connla again. Conn again summons his Druid to protect his son, but this time fails. In Joyce, the maiden chants several verses to Connla in this mode:

A pleasant land of winding vales, bright streams,
    and verdurous plains,
Where summer all the live-long year, in change-
    less splendour reigns:
A peaceful land of calm delight, of everlasting
    bloom;
Old age and death we never know, no sickness,
    care, or gloom;
The land of youth,
Of love and truth,
From pain and sorrow free;
The land of rest,
In the golden west,
On the verge of the azure sea!

Connla then joins her in a "gleaming, straight-gliding, strong, crystal canoe" and they sail out of sight to the "utmost verge," Connla never to be seen again in his land.[6]

In the Cousins' play formed from this story, the encounter of Connla and Conn with the Fairy Princess is a single encounter, with the power of the King's Druid overcome; the wondrous apple is eliminated. Conn sleeps, "weary of the sound of harp and song, and hungers for great peace" as the Princess appears to lure him. She identifies herself:

I am the lonely one amid the throng;
I am the royal beggar at the door
Of hushed and listening hearts. Among the dew
At dawn I wander, and at eve I breathe
On upturned faces round the fires of men.
I have a throne among the ageless stars,
And with the waving grass and fluttering moth,
And with the infant smile on aged lips
And with the immortal dreams of mortal hearts. (19)

A representative personification of the land of eternal perfection that recurs in the verse and drama of the Irish Renaissance, especially in the early Yeats, her dialogue is in the languid lushness of that kind. Cousins has a fairy chorus sing, suggesting the perfection of the initial creative essence:

The sun dropped down the sky, and fell
Into a golden crucible,

> From which uprolled
> Clouds flushed with fire that curved and curled,
> And we shook them, and flooded half the world
>   With gold. (17)

Connla feels himself drawn by the eternal presence of the Princess.
He dimly recalls her in his dreamy, but spiritual past:

> I think that face has touched my dreams
> With silver light, and drawn my being's tide;
> . . . .
> And beckoned me across a tranquil sea
> Into the golden glories of a dawn
> Beyond the tides of death and birth, and sleep.
> . . . .
> O voice that often whispered from the stars!
> O eyes that looked from dim fantastic caves!
> O arms that I have felt about the world!
> Now do I see thee, hear thee, now possess
> Exultant as high noon. (18)

She dismisses her fairy retinue so that she can be alone with
Connla:

>   . . . Away, ye twilight ones,
> Shake now the Branch of Night, and let its bells
> Tremble with music, til the souls of men
> Bloom upward thro' the soil of Sleep and flower
> And fructify in gardens no man tills. (19)

Her mission is also to bring men's souls to perfection, to beauty.
Connla is enthralled and falls immediately in love. He follows as she
beckons. King Conn awakes and he and his Druid, Coran, entreat
Connla to stay. Connla rejects Conn's crown, to follow his vision:

> Her throne shall hear no power-proud King; her King
> Shall mount no perilous throne amid decay.
> Her throne is with all changeless things,
> And with the everlasting stars. (26)

The fairy chorus chants to distant harps as Connla joins his Princess.
Thus, for Cousins, the story signifies his philosophical outlook:

the universe began at perfect unity, fragmented into the earthly and human reality of Connla, and is being drawn back to the initial perfect unity of the Fairy Maiden. Connla, in joining the Fairy Princess, goes onto the eternal tide to the realm in store for all the earth and all its inhabitants.

The play is delicate and evanescent, with a mood nowhere disturbed in the telling. There are some lines of lovely fantasy describing the kingdom of the Fairy Princess, who, like the vision in Shelley's *Alastor* and the voices in Yeats' "The Stolen Child," lures Connla away. There is not, however, the counterbalancing regret over the loss of the realm of earthly reality as in "The Stolen Child" and "The Wanderings of Oisin" of Yeats. The spirit realm is complete beauty and completely satisfying for Cousins, as for Shelley, and there is no trace of tragic conflict here. King Conn, in his old age and in his failure to hold his son, is merely touching and sad in his ineffectiveness. In this, we can find the primary failing of this play: there is no essential dramatic conflict, no drama. The play has a poetic pageantry about it, but it would have been as successful as one of Cousins' poetic narratives on legendary subject matter, which is basically what it is, with some delicate poetic lines telling of the primary spiritual perfection. For Cousins, the play was a vehicle of expression of his "inborn intuitive relationship of my inner self with the nature and technique of the universe."[7]

The play was staged in 1902, by the Irish National Dramatic Company with Frank Fay as King Conn and the Irish actress, Maire Nic Shuibhlaigh, as the Fairy Princess,[8] and it received short reviews dismissing it as "a picturesque little allegory,"[9] or "a charming little one-act play in verse" that would have benefited by being played behind a gauze curtain as Russell's *Deirdre* had been.[10]

II   The Sword of Dermot

Cousins' longer, three-act play, *The Sword of Dermot*, dramatized a legend current in various forms in County Roscommon. There, Cousins visited the original scene of the story and went to the grave of the play's two lovers, where it had been said "two trees twined themselves into a true lovers' knot over their tomb." He wrote that he "saw the tomb, but not the trees." The story haunted him with "a sweet sorrow" and he studied the manners and customs of the period for use in the play, although his efforts to produce an archaic speech are faltering:

Aedh of the tripping tongue has brought with him his poet staves that are cut with mirthmaking tales of Erinn. I have come out of the midst of their laughter to seek you. [11]

The play was produced successfully by the National Literary Society in April, 1903, after Cousins had been "snuffed out" of the Irish National Dramatic Company by Yeats. [12] Joseph Holloway felt Cousins had "reason to be proud of the reception given to his graceful, dainty, and beautifully-worded romantic little Irish play." [13]

The play is not as good as its reception suggests. It presents star-crossed lovers, Una and Owen, and is heavy with talk of prophecy, fate, and tragic inevitability, much of it centering on the sword of Dermot, which has been passed from Dermot to his son Bryan, Una's father. To preserve peace in the kingdom, Bryan commands Una to marry Fergal, but she refuses, since she loves Owen, the son of the enemy of the kingdom, to whom she is drawn by universal tides in the same manner that Connla is attracted by the Fairy Princess in *The Sleep of the King*. Una expresses it thus:

I come from the eternities to this hour. The Son of Costello [Owen] came into my sky with eternities glimmering in his wake; the eternal flowed and mingled in our first secret kiss; and the eternal shall wither and split, like an unsung and forgotten poet stave before I forget, or he. (3)

The king opposes the union, and war ensues, which brings the death of his children—his son Cahil and his daughter Una—as well as of Owen, who dies by the corpse of Una, speaking his last words:

> Come, Una. Usheen awaits his beautiful bride—
> And together they went away
> To the Land of the Ever Young. (3)

All of the action of the play has been the working-out of a prophecy which has brought otherworldly forces into the play and the dialogue. The play does not succeed as tragedy. Dissolving in a moody sadness, the play is another vehicle for Cousins' Theosophical views. Years later, in India, he composed a poetic version of the play which was published in a magazine in Madras. [14]

III   A Man's Foes *and* Sold

A Cousins' play performed in the same year, on November 3, 1903, has apparently been lost, since it never reached publication. The play, *A Man's Foes*, was reviewed, however, and one of the reviews reveals the plot, centered on a painter's drinking problem. The painter embraces abstinence, but his sweetheart's father, a wealthy whiskey manufacturer, commissions the artist to paint a whiskey bottle poster. The model bottle destroys the painter and his potential marriage. Then he apparently clarifies for the audience that a man's foes are really all in his own mind.[15] Although the play brought some praise in 1903, seemingly in the same style as the play: "It is a little picture, of which we cannot crumple a corner without spoiling the whole,"[16] it can probably be dismissed as a moralistic melodrama of temporary worth.

Sold[17] is the play Yeats felt was rubbish. Cousins' only attempt at comedy, it is a two-act play of complex pretenses—including pretended death—and complications and cross-purposes over the supposed foreclosure of a farm. The overhearings, mishearings, and plotting produce farcical confusions, and a dialogue full of quick patter, jests, and puns. The play is a new tone for Cousins, and the only place in all his writings that we find any evidence of attempted humor. While not distinctive nor deftly subtle, there is some adequately funny silliness, ably managed. There is some Northern dialect and vocabulary in the play. It saw its only production in Cork in December, 1902,[18] for Yeats effectively kept it away from Dublin.

IV   The Turn of the Tide *and*
The Racing Lug

Cousins' two sea plays, on the other hand, reveal a turn toward realism. *The Turn of the Tide*[19] is the lesser of the two plays, and the later: it was written in 1905 and marked the end of its author's interest in playwriting in Dublin. The play has apparently never been produced. It is a one-act play set in the 1870s in a Northern Ireland fishing village. The action of the sea enters the play as it affects the two love stories of the contrived plot, by drowning simultaneously, at moments of heroism, two people, each of whom is the third party in two love-triangle pursuits on shore. The two go to their deaths willingly, giving themselves up for the love and happiness of their beloved. The one interesting love relationship of the two is that of Captain Henderson, an aged widowed seaman, for the young Meg, who reminds him of his dead wife. Captain Henderson's travels had brought him to India, he tells Meg, where he learned of souls passing from one body to another; he wonders if Meg has the soul of his former wife. Actually, Meg loves the captain's son and her love is returned. The captain heroically gives up his life saving stranded people from a sinking barque. A storm is coming, the tide turns, and the captain is swept away in the act of saving lives.

The theme of love and giving of self for love is strongly evident, as a result of the contrivance in the plot and direct compressed shifts in conversational groups to present the two love triangles. The play is ultimately weak melodrama.

The speedily written *The Racing Lug*[20] is Cousins' most successful play, although his first. Composed in one morning, it reflects the kind of theater called for by Lady Gregory:

Any knot of events, where there is passionate emotion and a dash of will, can be made the subject matter of a play, and the less like a play it is at the first sight the better the play may come of it in the end. Young writers should remember that they must get all their effects from the logical expression of their subject and not by the addition of extraneous incidents.[21]

Cousins' later plays are over-contrived and overstated, perhaps the victims of the over-zealous workmanship which was a detriment to his poetic utterances as well. But this was not so of the earlier *The Racing Lug*. The play was written at Frank Fay's request and produced in 1902 by the Irish National Theatre Society, with Yeats' approval. It was also the inaugural performance of the Theatre of Ireland company. It opened in Molesworth Hall on December 6, 1906; George Moore, Lady Gregory, Padraic Colum, Douglas Hyde, and George Sigerson were in the audience.[22]

The play is set in the cottage kitchen of a seaman, Johnny, of a Northern Ireland fishing village in the 1880s. His wife, Nancy, is reading the Bible and his daughter, Bell, is cleaning up as the play begins; the young Presbyterian minister, showing interest in Bell, arrives to pay a call. The minister speaks of Rob, a young fisherman who, unknown to the group, is Bell's love. Rob plans to put the huge sail, the racing lug, on his boat and to put out to sea in the current lull between storms. Rob then appears and Johnny as a wise seaman tries, unsuccessfully, to dissuade him. When Rob and Bell are left alone for a moment in the kitchen, they embrace, only to be discovered by Johnny. An angry discourse follows with Rob, who rashly retorts that at least he's not a coward about putting out to sea with the racing lug. Provoked by that challenging insult, Johnny sets off with Rob to put to sea as the storm brews. The second scene is two hours later in the cottage, as the two women wait for the return of their men. The minister arrives with the sad news that the boat has been swamped and that Rob lives, but that Johnny is dead. Nancy, Johnny's wife, slumps slowly in her chair when she hears the news. Rob, feeling responsible for Johnny's death, appears and falls disconsolate into Bell's embrace. The minister moves towards the dead Nancy as the play ends.

The shortness of the play and the single simple setting intensifies the dramatic character of the play. The dialogue, a Northern dialect, is a natural, authentic, and genuine one that conveys a realistic grip to the events, the emotions, and the characters. Nowhere else in Cousins are there such realistic human beings so feelingly depicted in their human weakness, frailty, and mortality. There is in the characterization and setting an ardent, earthly humanness that is absent from his verse and other plays. These are living human beings enduring their earthly lot. As the play is constructed and moves, the audience is made to feel the growing presence of the coming disaster and then its fearsome effects and pathetic wake.

The play brings to mind Synge's *Riders to the Sea*, the greatest Irish sea play, which was started by Synge the following summer of 1902 and first produced in 1904. It is difficult not to think of Cousins' play as an influence on or a catalyst to Synge's great drama, though Synge's play is far superior to *The Racing Lug* and though no recorded data remains to confirm that Synge was aware of Cousins' play. Nevertheless, we have the same basic setting in each play—the cottage kitchen which becomes the scene of the realization of the inevitable death exacted by the sea. The characters' motivations to go down to the sea in spite of the foreboding differ, however. In *Riders to the Sea*, Bartley must go; it is a way of life and livelihood: thus there is a tragic conflict between man and the universe. In *The Racing Lug*, Johnny goes to sea out of insult and anger; he could more wisely have remained home: thus there is only a melodramatic event and the tragedy of human folly. Synge's play penetrates to the soul of its characters; Cousins' play seeks out the heart and feeling. The greatness of Synge's play is the

spiritual height it reaches and the splendor it reveals in humble people. The distinctiveness in Cousins' play is in his presentation of
true feeling for human emotion and real human beings in realistic
circumstances.

Cousins' interest in playwriting in Dublin lasted only three years,
though it was to return briefly in India. His Dublin efforts resulted
in melodrama, farce, and verse drama. The mood ranged from
mythological fantasy lyrically told with philosophical connotation,
to folk farce, to melodrama of human emotion evoked when man
encounters the insuperable forces of hostile nature. In each there is
notable workmanship. One play, *The Racing Lug*, deserves not to
be forgotten and could be successfully presented at any time and
place. *The Sleep of the King* will always be important because of its
significant position in the development of the Irish drama.

V   *Plays Written in India*

Cousins' interest in drama emerged again in 1919 in India. In
that year, he worked on a poetical version of his Irish play of 1903,
The Sword of Dermot, and the new version was published in
Shama'a, a Madras magazine.[23] Also in 1919, Cousins' totally new
play, *The King's Wife*, first appeared. This, too, was later revised
and retitled *Mira of Mewar*. It remains unpublished and un-
produced.[24] *The King's Wife* is a dramatic telling of an Indian tale
of a meeting of the Hindu Queen Mirabai, a renowned poetess and
saint of the latter fifteenth century, and the Mughal Emperor Akbar
of the latter sixteenth century, whose reign is studded with major
accomplishments, including an attempt to create an eclectic religion
for India. Since the two lives are separated by a century, the play
romanticizes their meeting, with Akbar, disguised as a Hindu, lured
by the music of Mirabai's singing. The disguised—and un-
recognized—Akbar, in admiration, gives her a necklace. The gift
outrages King Kumbha, the Queen's husband. He passes a death
sentence on the Queen but she escapes, dressed as a beggar — a
Queen with the walk of a beggar, the opposite of Yeats' Cathleen ni
Houlihan, an old woman with the walk of a Queen.

The verse of the play contains some of the unfortunate metaphors
of which Cousins is capable:

> I hear the tap, tap, tap
> Of some woodpecker at the tree of life,

> Shredding its bark until the shrinking flesh
> Is bare to wind and rain, and rottenness
> Creeps up its bole and feeds on leaf and flower.
> Oh! that tree's fall will bring a kingdom's fruit
> Into the dust. (142)

But there is, as in Cousins' verse, a calm Tennysonian tone in some lines:

> The Queen comes now to worship, and may bring
> A song to God, new budded on the lake
> Of her calm soul; a lotus in the dawn,
> That smiles to heaven, but holds a shining tear,
> Oh! she has brought strange quiet on the world,
> The exquisite sadness of things beautiful
> That is more sweet than laughter. (115)

The Queen makes explicit the Cousins philosophy:

> But underneath the surface
> We may be different; and deeper still
> Be no more different than that great Life
> That comes and goes, that feeds and sings and prays,
> And is, ah! slowly slowly, gathered home
> By the awakened soul. (125)

And one of the secondary characters gives voice to Cousins' creative aim:

> I count no poet worthy of the craft
> Whose aim is not pitched higher than the highest. (111)

The play is one mainly of mood and tone, with the dramatic action and dramatic conflict subordinated. The poetic craft in the verse is to suggest awareness, by the way of the tone, of the "great Life" that weaves through the life of man. The facts of history are altered in an attempt to present that greater reality.

The Hound of Uladh[25] is the result of a decade of effort, from 1932 to 1942, "to give through the free imagination an interpretation of one of the major tales of the Irish mythos, 'The Exile of the Sons of Doel Dermait,' "[26] and marks in Cousins a return of the impulse to write verse dramas about Irish mythology. Work on it was begun on Anacapri on the return journey after lecturing on Irish

poetry in New York City. Cousins saw in his development of the
Cuchulain story what he felt to be Cuchulain's "culmination as the
perfect spiritual initiate, the 'Saviour Hero' of the unintimidated
Celtic imagination."[27] Cousins called the work a "mythological fantasy," not "in the fantastic sense, but in the classical sense of making the invisible visible through the imagination" (ix), and he used
his separately published poem, "Bricriu - Bitter - Tongue,"[28] as a
prologue, thus bringing the Feast of Bricriu story and the Doel Dermait story together in his work, and using them as symbolic of
"moral and spiritual conditions" by his own "creative imagination
and intuition" (69), to "catch the inner import of the myths . . . "
and "to tell it as truly and musically as I could" (71). This central
import Cousins also saw in Indian myth, for "the realities which the
old Celtic deities symbolized were eternally valid both in the constants of universal life and in the flux of human concepts of that life
from religion to religion and era to era" (71). Cuchulain, then, is the
Irish parallel to the Hindu Atman, the divine spark, the Will; Laeg,
Cuchulain's charioteer, is Krishna, the receptacle of knowledge and
intuition that carries Will to fulfillment; Lugaidh, the knight-
compatriot of Cuchulain in the play, is Monas, the active Mind that
adjusts external details to fulfillment,[29] as they become explicitly
defined in the play.
     Cousins develops Findchoem, the woman who attracts and is at-
tracted by Cuchulain, beyond the details of her character in the
myth story. She becomes

> a pioneer of womanhood, a worthy comrade of
> Maeve of Cruachan who was as potent a queen
> as any man was King, and of Dechtere, the
> mother of Cuchulain, who was the charioteer
> of her brother, King Conchubar of Uladh. (74)

     The development of Findchoem's stature is another manifesta-
tion of the equality of the sexes and the dualism of power in the universe, which also emerges in another way in the work. Cuchulain's
"double parentage from the Sun-God Lugh and the earthly prince
Sualtam," with Lugh as a spirit father and Sualtam as a body father,
is representative of "the ancient recognition of the cooperative an-
tagonism that runs through all life from its highest to its lowest
forms" (77).
     Cousins' continuing interest in expressing the eternal essence in

the temporal reality, frequently using metaphor in verse, deter-
mines the dramatic form of this work: the action takes place in the
mythological realm and in Dublin of 1911, with the three main
characters in Dublin representing modern manifestations of the
three mythological figures, Cuchulain, Laeg, and Lugaidh. Bricriu's
introduction is directly addressed to the modern audience and he
brings them to the past of mythology, the "stable centre" Cousins
calls it; then Bricriu becomes a character in the action of the past, as
the Red Branch Knights of Irish myth are introduced. Cuchulain
charges off with Laeg and Lugaidh to free the imprisoned sons of
Doel Dermait. Enroute, he and Findchoem are drawn together.

> She lived a life within a world of dreams,
> And through the threnody of transient things
> Heard the far harps of immortality,
> And fortified herself on secret love
> That found disguise and utterance in song. (101)

Her appearance is followed by one of the several lyric interludes.
Cuchulain, she says,

> . . . rides above the moods of men
> Dealing the high decrees of doom;
> Flashing from sky to sod
> The splendour of a God. (116)

As in Cousins' early writings, with their lovers, Daghda and Dana,
and Etain and Mider, the beauty of the verse of love's anticipation
is followed by insipid verse detailing the consummation of the love.
It is difficult to ignore the biographical facts of the Cousins'
marriage. As in Cousins' life, the idea of loving is better than the act
of loving.

The next scene shifts to Brigid, Aedh, and Blanaid, the servants of
the sons of Doel Dermait on the Island of Captivity, who reveal in
undramatic conversation the arrival of Cuchulain and the setting
free of the three sons. The verse in this section is the least good, being merely measured prose. The reality of modern Dublin, called
the "City of Dreams," to clarify its transience in relation to the
realm of myth, becomes the scene of the next section—specifically,
in a Dublin lodging-house. Cuchulain in this manifestation is called
Dumb Dog (as Hound of Uladh), Laeg (as charioteer) is called
Horsey, and Lughaidh (since he sees three sides to every question)

is Double Shuffle. They talk in modern idiom and refer to Trinity
College, O'Connell Street, the Ancient Concert Rooms, Gaiety
Theatre, and the smell of Liffey. Also, getting more specific in
Cousins' connections, they speak of the suffragettes, Sheehy-
Skeffington, AE, the Fays, a play about Prince Connla of the
Golden Hair, and Hinduism. The dialogue is filled with remarks
and sometimes jibes about life in contemporary Dublin, theoretical-
ly from the Olympian view of the gods, but actually from the point
of view of Cousins. The three characters are viewed as crazy by the
Dubliners, but as the scene ends, a figure appears and speaks, saying "My God . . . supposing it was true?" (198), recalling the end
of Yeats' play, "The Resurrection."

The last two scenes return to the mythological realm for the
depiction of Cuchulain's triumphant return from combat to find his
food still fresh and untasted, signifying that his "long quest" had
actually been, in Cousins' explanation, a "moment of the ecstatic
opening of his eyes to what I conceived to be the major Mystery of
life—the Mystery of fixity in motion, of eternal within the temporal" (73). Cuchulain then joins Findchoem at Cruachan of the
Bards, and they take their places with the Irish hierarchy, Maeve,
Etain, and Mider. The "mythological fantasy" draws to a close with
an evening chant to Lugh, including the verse,

> One is thy gift to man and beast,
> To opening leaf and folded wing;
> Day for life's labour and for feast,
> And night for rich remembering. (270)

And Bricriu assures the audience

> . . . that all things undeflected move
> Through ill to well in life's ascending groove. (270)

While Cousins had held fast to his idealistic philosophy, his lyric
gift had weakened, and the evanescent moods and scenes that he
could previously create in "Etain the Beloved" and "Connla of the
Golden Hair" are not here. The realistic conversations in Dublin,
complaining about injustice for women, unfairness, the middle
class' lack of appreciation for art and things of the spirit, all serve to
disjoint the play and its theme of upward evolution. Incoherent in
tone, the play's idealism is unconvincing. The emotional heightening of the earlier Cousins' fantasies of the realistic invisible is lack-

ing. The work does not, as Cousins in his Shelley-like way had hoped, enlighten and reveal an eternal reality and realm of calm and peace. The effort was there, however, and the work was long in maturing, for Cousins gave

the best days and nights of the seventh decade of this life (1932-42) to bringing together, in this mythological fantasy, Celtic myth and English poetry, under the insistence of a vision that had to fulfill itself in utterance, though a lifetime lay between its burgeoning among "the far hills of holy Ireland" and its flowering and fruiting on and between the equally fair hills of a not less holy India. (78)

Drama (surpassed in value only by poetry for Cousins) he regarded highly because it possessed "the highest synthetical power," and synthesis, as he defined it, was a major goal of his thinking, especially in his India years. Drama knocked "simultaneously at all doors," he said, and he outlined its significance in national revival in *The Play of Brahma: An Essay on the Drama in National Revival.* The stage in India could, he thought, "enrich the national consciousness and and emotion"[30] as it had in Ireland, for the drama is "rooted in order" and moves "in lines of divergence and convergence towards fulfillment" (14). In 1921, Cousins felt, "If Ireland had been left to the dramatists, things would be different now" (14) because the Irish dramatic revival "knew the high joy of the discovery of the soul, though in chains, and the power of the immortal self over the limitations of matter" (10). "All India must walk the stage," he exhorted, just as Yeats had said, "All Ireland must walk the stage" (10), and Cousins advised Indians to develop a knowledge of their dramatic history, to foster an observance of dramatic unity in playwriting, and to forsake the Oriental custom of all-male stage in finding, through drama, a view of the proportion and balance in life. Drama was, he held, a miniature of the universal process (6).

CHAPTER 4

The Poetry

POETRY, for Cousins, surpassed other literary forms, and it is in this genre that his most sustained literary talent and thought found expression. Essentially self-taught in literary matters, Cousins read widely and sensitively, especially in English and Irish poetry. Perhaps as a result of his independent education, much of Cousins' verse is often derivative, as he experimented in his own efforts to emulate the variety of forms and meters that he admired in his reading. Traces of the stylistic traits of Shakespeare, Shelley, Keats, and Tennyson can be discerned in Cousins' verse, along with influences from his contemporaries, especially Yeats and AE. Like so many Irish poets, in his years in Ireland he drew heavily on Ireland for his subject matter—on its myths, its past, and its natural beauty. Also, as is frequent in Irish verse, Cousins' poetry often relied upon a specific place—a particular mountain, town, stream, etc.—for its subject or its controlling image using it to reflect his larger purpose. The wide range of verse form to be found in his work itself reflects Cousins' untiring efforts in attempting a variety of molds within which he could express the Theosophical view that controlled his perceptions and was the continuing theme of his poetic writing. In his earlier creative years he wrote a considerable body of longer narrative and mythological poems.

I Long Poems

A. Legendary Narratives: Belfast

Early in his poetic career, while still in Belfast, Cousins, in the spirit of the Celtic Renaissance, was drawn to stories of the Irish past. This attraction also provided the subject matter for a number of long narrative poems written mostly in Cousins' Dublin years, and the basis for other, later poems touching on myth.

The pagan-Christian conflict is the central issue in Cousins' first

narrative poem, "Ben Madighan," written in 1894—which deals
with early legendary material about the mountain, Ben Madighan,
near Belfast (on which, too, the patriots Wolfe Tone, Thomas
Russell, and Samuel Nelson had later vowed at the time of the 1798
uprising to struggle for Ireland's freedom). The legend of the poem
is the story Cousins used for his play, *The Clansman*, discussed in
the preceding chapter, of the struggle between two warring clans,
Savage and Mac Gilmore. The poem makes a poor attempt at im-
itating Keats: the prelude, in blank verse couplets, includes the
lines,

> Oh!—for a draught from that Castalian fount
> Which ripples from Parnassus' sacred mount,
>
> . . .
>
> To warm my breast and tune my loftiest lyre!
> To sing to thee, whose inspiration thrills
> True patriot's heart, dear native vales and hills![1]

The poem's First Canto of twenty stanzas begins the poem in
Spenserian stanza. The remainder of the poem is written in iambic
tetrameter couplets, in stanzas of varying length. The opening canto
shows, too, the influence of the vocabulary and the sentimentality
of late eighteenth century verse, reinforced by rhymed couplets.
The poet stands at the peak of Ben Madighan so that his soul might
"View with delighted eye and pulsing heart/ Scenes it might dream
of; scenes all but Divine!" (27). The scenes are humble, rural ones;
the busy City where "commerce rules" is in the distance. The poet
has gone when "Day is declining in the golden West" (24), and
presently night arrives, stars shine, and "Soon o'er the dark horizon
Luna springs" (33). The poet is lifted out of the moment: "In
thought I'm carried back to days of yore;/ I see the smoke of battle
Heavenward curl;/ I see war's flag its blood-stained folds unfurl;"
(33). The remaining two cantos relate the story of the struggle
between the Savage and Mac Gilmore clans as seen by the poet in a
near-vision. The enmity is caused by the sister of a Savage running
away with a Mac Gilmore and living with him, unblessed by the
Church. In the struggle of the Christian Savages and the pagan Mac
Gilmores, the girl is accidentally killed by an arrow shot by her
brother. The vision of the events told by the poet fades as the poem
ends with mention of other people and events in the lore of the
mountain. The last stanza is a series of trite farewells by the poet to
the glades, crags, streams, and caves of the mountain. This early

poem, imitative, conventional, and uninteresting, contains no
notable verse, but shows a firm and disciplined attempt at verse
form, variety of stanzaic pattern, and meter.

"The Legend of the Blemished King," published in 1897, con-
cerns the legend of King Fergus. The source was the Reverend
James Laverty's *The Ecclesiastical History of Down and Connor*.
Cousins' rendering shifts from the historical realism of "Ben
Madighan." King Fergus, when asleep, is awakened by a group of
fairy elves. When he captures three of them, and they plead for
their lives, he strikes a bargain with them: "Through the deep/ And
under, give me knowledge of the way,/ Unfearful of the power of
wave or spray."[2] The fairies grant the knowledge, on the condition
that Fergus stay away from Lough Rory (Dundrum Bay), which is
beyond human scope. Fergus receives his powers as the fairies
"plant sweet spices, herbs anointing clear" (28). He uses his new
abilities to explore the deep, but Fergus wants, predictably, to do
the forbidden, to descend into Rory: "Fergus is Fergus still—and
Fergus knows no fear!" (31). He descends to see sea flowers, rocks,
some drowned bodies, and finally to confront a dreadful shape,
Muirdis, a fiend and ogre. Fergus, in fear, flees to the beach, col-
lapsing, dazed and limp, with a blemish on his face marking his forbidden expedition and fearful flight. His charioteer, Muena, carries
his unconscious body to the Council of the Kingdom to plead for
the impeachment. "King Fergus, from Ambition evil-starred,/ Lies
now before your eyes in visage sorely scarred." (37). The Council,
however, votes confidence in Fergus and decrees that no one tell
him of his facial blemish. Three years pass, with Fergus in ignorance of the scar, until he learns of it by chance. He returns to
Rory to prove himself, and tremendous waves well up as the people
of the kingdom wait at water's edge for the decision of the epic battle below, just as the decision of Beowulf's epic battle with
Grendel's mother was awaited. The water goes bloody red and
Fergus appears above water without his blemish. He claims his vic-
tory, but anounces, as he sinks back into the water forever, "I but
pay the price of mine own deed." (48).

In this poem of forty-eight stanzas, Cousins manages to sustain
his use of the Spenserian stanza. The narrative moves in a steady
pace with notably good focus on the significant events, and the
poem is devoid of tangential and superfluous digressions. The attention to those waiting on shore rather than to the second encounter
of Fergus with Muirdis neatly piques the imagination and builds fit-

ting suspense. But the poem is the work of an immature poet improving his narrative style and is otherwise not noteworthy.

B. *Mythological Narratives: Dublin*

Cousins' volume, *The Quest,* published in 1906 in Dublin, contained two Irish mythological narratives, "The Going Forth of Dana" and "The Marriage of Lir and Niav," each showing Cousins' Theosophical interpretation of myth. In the first, Dana and Dagda, clarified by Cousins as the mother of the Irish Gods and the Zeus of Irish mythology, go forth from the Nameless One, Dana scattering seed that "flamed in gold of heavy corn" and ignoring a Shadow that passes over her, begging her to rest. She must continue "that Spring may thus endure,"[3] and the Shadow, then, joins her efforts. Together, they entice flowers to spring up—violets, pansies, hyacinths, and marigolds. Not all of the poetry brings this about felicitously. Note, for example, what Cousins did to the humble cowslip: "The Cowslip's little rocket skyward shot,/ And earthward fell in throbbing yellow stars." (4)

Dagda appears when Dana has stopped her work. Spring has passed, and harvest is at hand. Dagda stoops to kiss his resting spouse, and a Voice thunders out: *"One for the Seed, and for the Sowing Twain./ But for the Ripening Three, for Reaping Seven,/ And seven times seven for the garnering."* (7) Dana weeps, and Dagda soothes her. There is need for help—for sons—for the reaping. Then a flash with a fiery spear comes from the East and touches Dana's forehead. A new scene presents Dana in a bower as seven names are murmured on the wind; Dana drinks from a stream, and the water flows through her fingers in a shower of seven rainbows. A silver-white Heron appears as Dana turns to the West, and,

> . . . Upon the Hills
> A passionate glory like a Lover lay,
> And stretched wild arms that burned across the sky
> And, closing round Her, clasped Her in a thrill
> Of Flaming ecstasy, so that her feet
> Weary no more, but swift with all Desire
> Flew like a glimmer of light along the grass,
> And vanished in the Flame upon the Hills. (11)

The poem then ends quickly with the murmur of Seven Names.

The poem is a presentation of Cousins' own belief of all creation emanating from and returning to a single perfect source—the Nameless One. Dagda and Dana—male and female—come from this source, and further fragmented manifestations follow. Dana, then, is lured back to the Nameless One as she turns to the West to the Lover who embraces her, with whom she is weary no more and with whom she vanishes. The significance of the poem is not clearly evident in the poem itself: a knowledge of Cousins' own philosophical point of view is needed by the reader, but even then there are vaguenesses and ambiguities. Why, for instance, doesn't the male, Dagda, return to his source? Is he forsaken? Or indeed, has he played any part in producing the seven sons, which may be the seven islands of the world? The use of the fiery flash comes very close to the Christian conception of Christ, and leaves Dagda an inept Zeus or an unproductive Joseph. The verse is undistinguished, reaching its nadir in lines similar to the lines above describing the cowslip.

The other narrative in *The Quest* is "The Marriage of Lir and Niav." Gretta and James Cousins both believed that Gretta, in a dream or trance, had received direct assistance for the poem from the spirit of Niav, an Irish mythological goddess who is a character in the poem. This narrative is written in over four hundred lines of blank verse. The identity and material about Lir, the father of Mananaun, the Irish god of the sea, comes from Standish O'Grady.[4] Lir, as lord of the seven seas that wash the seven islands of the world, Eire being the chief island, has grown weary of years, harvests, and pleasures, and expresses his weariness in a fashion reminiscent of early Tennyson (particularly his *Ulysses*):

> What profits me this affluence? What avails
> This peace that slumbers on its rusted harp
> For lack of song? What joy is in the chant
> Of What is done, save when it nerves the arm
> Of those who do? for doing is all in all. (30)

Consequently, Lir considers sailing forth, but is advised in alliterative and onomatopoetic lines, "to wait a settled wind,/ And take the stride of long unanimous waves/ With strong, slow swing of sure and steady oars." (31-32) Another adviser wisely suggests he take a bride from his islands. Soon, Lir sleeps and dreams, "Of One who bent/ And touched his brow with lips of silvery fire" (33), and when Lir awakes words pass through his mind as an echo to his dream advising him to take a bride. The words bring him a sense of connection with some essence in a previous existence. Cousins explains that the words had awakened in Lir,

> . . . a tender dream
> So vague, so far beyond the misty verge
> Of time and sense, that to his ear it came
> Like some sweet echo of a chant of love
> Heard once before the gates of Birth had closed
> Upon the Music that has built the worlds. (34)

Lir then sails seven times seven leagues to "a land as fair as the fairest dream," in which there is the "royal house of him whose mighty name/ May not be told till First and Last are one." (35) The house shines as a pearl in permanent radiance. Harpers play, as in Gretta's dream. Lir stands apart and receives the song of the harps

> . . . with tremors of a strange delight
> As tho' the song were sung for one He had loved
> Some other where beyond the gates of sleep.
> Then, when the mingled joy of all that throng
> Stood pinnacled upon the utmost height
> Of ecstasy, there fell a tremulous hush
> As if the parted lips of all the worlds
> Waited the word to hurl the highest heaven.

and then appearing "in that throbbing pause/ Came Niav, daughter of the King whose name/ May not be named till First and Last are one." (36-37) Lir gazes on her, and Cousins chooses sea imagery for the description. Her clothes, "white as foam," are hung with a "sea-green girdle," which is like "mermaid weed," and "within her wake/ There came the sound and odour of the sea." (37) Lir is affected, the movement and sound of the sea again providing apt imagery: "the surging tides/ Of all His being mingled with the tide/ Of Love that moved across the ecstatic throng/ And bent and broke about her, as a sea." (37-38) Male and female eddy and well within the engulfing sea and are swept together and merged in the greater. Niav has sensed that someone is coming who "has sent His dream before Him," and then she sees Lir "and knew, and trembled" (40). From this point, the quality of the poem deteriorates, and the culmination of the love is disappointing and ineffectively narrated.

Lir takes Niav to his ship and they sail "amid a shout of triumph homeward," where they pass "thro' white Love from peace to peace" (47). Mananaun the sea god is born, and receives the crown when grown and strong.

The outlook of Cousins is more clearly and more beautifully set forth here than in "The Going Forth of Dana." The element of the unknowable pre-existence and goal is here, most emphatically stated with Niav's father as a "King whose name may not be named till First and Last are one." The union of First and Last is similar to the holy marriage of each of the holy entities, the male Lir, and the female Niav. The offspring, the god of the sea, has a dual divine origin.

The narrative has some very good lyrical passages as it moves, as a contemporary reviewer said, through "astral essences into a web of occultism impossible for mere intellectual penetration."[5] Shelley's idealism and Tennyson's expression are imitated. There is a conventional control of rhythm, intensified by the imitation of expression. The plot develops with an obvious inevitability. The poem seldom if ever produces any vitality. No matter how delicate and melodious the smoothly flowing lines are, as they reveal higher powers moving through life toward the consummate ending, the lifeless quality is always there. Drama and originality of expression are lacking, caused by Cousins' reverent imitation and unquestionable convictions. The subjectivity of thought, instead of being conveyed in concrete but appropriate imagery as in Shelley, or as in the enormously exaggerated realities of Milton, is impotently spoken in vague terms.

"Etain the Beloved," the title poem of his 1912 volume of verse published in Dublin, is by far Cousins' best narrative, in development, in interpretation, and in poetic technique. About this poem, he later said, "in technique I had got the nearest of any of the movement to the versual distinction of the Bards, and had caught, and developed, some of their ideas of individual and super-human life."[6] Cousins found the Etain story in its orginal form in *The Irish Mythological Cycle and Celtic Mythology* of 1903, by H. d'Arbois de Jubainville,[7] whose richly informative work had provided a major channel for Irish mythology to direct its impact on writers in English. The essence of the story in de Jubainville is this: Etain, the wife of the god Mider, is abducted, and through a series of marvelous events and adventures is at last restored to Mider. The separation begins when Mider's pupil and foster son carries Etain away and marries her, staying with her in a "chamber filled with sweet smelling flowers." Mider's second wife, jealous of her husband's lingering love for Etain, arouses a wind which blows through Etain's room and carries her to the roof of a great mansion in which Ulster's noblemen and their wives are feasting. Etain falls through the chimney and lands in a drinking cup. One of the women drinks from the cup, and swallows Etain, thereby becomeing impregnated. Etain is reborn. At rebirth, Etain is twelve hundred years old, "but the gods grow not old," as de Jubainville points out (177).

When Etain matures, she marries the high king at Tara, Eochaid Airem, who is said to be a contemporary of Caesar the Great. Mider's love for Etain continues, however, and leads him to present himself to the new Etain. He identifies himself as her husband in the realm of the gods and beseeches her to return with him. Etain refuses, but Mider does not give up. Later, he returns to Tara in the dazzling array of a superior warrior. When Etain's husband Eochaid Airem greets him, Mider announces that he has come to play chess with Eochaid Airem, who is known as the best chess player in all of Ireland. Mider produces a silver chess-board decorated with jewels and sets out players of pure gold. Mider sets the stakes at whatever the winner demands. Eochaid is defeated, to his astonishment, and Mider demands Etain as his prize. Eochaid requests a second match in a year for the final determination. Mider agrees.

In that year, Mider appears to Etain numerous times and sings a song to her—a song that de Jubainville believed to be inappropriate, the result of an error by a scribe in antiquity. The song is that which the messenger of death sings, as he bears a woman to her immortal sojourn. Cousins, however, did not think the song misplaced. Mider, in de Jubainville, sings thus to Etain:

> O fair one, wilt thou come with
> me to a wonderful land that is
> mine, a land of sweet music;
> there primrose blossoms on
> the hair, and snow-white
> bodies from head to toe;
> there no one is sorrowful
> or silent; white teeth there,
> black the eyebrows . . .
> the hue of the foxglove is
> on every cheek . . . Though

> fair are the plains of
> Innisfail, few there are so
> fair as the Great Plain
> whither I call thee. The
> ale of Innisfail is heady,
> but headier far the ale of
> the Great Land. What a
> wonder of a land that
> is! No youth grows
> there to old age. (179 - 80)

De Jubainville felt this song misplaced, because Mider wished to return Etain to the land which had been familiar to her for several centuries, not to where men gathered after death. Cousins was not disturbed by it, though, for his philosophical system held that the beneficent point of origin for humans was also the ultimate goal to which they returned.

Even with the song and entreaty of Mider, Etain remains faithful to her husband at Tara. As the year agreed upon ends, Mider returns to Tara for the second chess game and to claim his rightful reward upon winning. He longs to put his two hands about the waist of Etain and kiss her. Eochaid delays one more month after his second loss, and bolsters his fortress against Mider's return. But Mider appears mysteriously among them on the appointed night, puts his two hands around Etain's waist, and rises into the air with her through the chimney hole. As Eochaid's warriors look up, they see two swans flying above Tara with their white necks linked by a band of silver. While Cousins stops his telling of the story here, de Jubainville's narrative goes on to tell that Eochaid later recovers Etain, and then Mider wreaks vengeance upon a later generation.

It is this story and its shifting incarnations—first in the realm of the gods, then in an earthly realm, and then again in the realm of the gods—that attracted Cousins. The relevance and influence of the story derived essentially from the view of the universe which Cousins saw embodied in the myth. The story, for Cousins, was perfect; it

set my imagination alight . . . with the vision of an embodiment of perfection forced by the decensive power in the universe from her original state as a consort of the King of Fairyland . . . to the outer state of wife to the King of Ireland; and being drawn back to the allurement of the mind to reunion with her true husband. Here was matter to my taste, the circle of the cosmic

life completed in a single story, and with a nearness to the details of nature
and of human psychology in its earthly phase that excited the imagination
with the anticipated delight of recreating the beauties of the temporal on
the background of the eternal.[8]

Cousins begins his poem in the temporal and earthly realm. As in
"The Marriage of Lir and Niav," the poem opens with a wifeless
King, Eochaid, who is entreated to seek a mate. He does so, urged
on by magical inspiration to his foreordained bride as he dozes by
the fire:

> Out of the fire a swift and slender shaft
> Of yellow flame pierced through the King's
> dropped lids,
>
> . . .
>
> At length in that white hour when dewy wings
> Stir with new day's delight, there came a sound
> As though a passion of voices and smitten strings
> Mingled and swelled and flew along the ground,
> Till at the utmost of its triumphings,
> Through the King's sleep and on his door the dawn
> Broke, and a mighty shout: "Etain! Etain!"[9]

In the second section of the poem, Etain appears, her beauty
described in a series of conventional similes. King Eochaid,
depicted frequently in animal similes, sees her, his heart "Strained
like a hound in leash," and proposes; she accepts, saying,

> . . . to thee my heart has bowed
> When minstrel after minstrel, tired and tanned,
> Has supped beside our hearth, and sung the proud
> High song that bears thy greatness through the land.
> For thee from life's clear dawn my love remained
> Fixed, and at length to thee I have attained. (13)

Marriage and a meeting with the King's brother, Ailill, whom
Cousins depicts as the God of Love, begins the third section. Ailill
immediately falls woefully in love with Etain and slowly sinks into
illness; Etain becomes his comfort and his nurse and, when the
King is on a long journey, his very pure consort and love. They
speak their love to one another, and as they do a song turns in
Etain's mind. The song tells how Strength, Life, Beauty, and Love
survive, while the strong, the alive, the beautiful, and the loving

die, a statement of Cousins' belief in eternal spiritual essences passing through transitory material entities. Etain then speaks, vaguely
knowledgeable of the levels of being her two men represent,

> King Eochaidh in his might
> Drew me to bonds of happiness; but thou
> Art as a voice that calls across the night
> To where some dawn blows freshly on the brow,
> And love with love moves freely as the light,
> Mingling in happy dreams their shadowy wings
> Beyond these perishing substantial things. (25)

Eochaid is an earthly lover; Ailill, beyond substantial things, is
spiritual love.

Human progression and destiny continue to unfold in the poem.
The progression for Etain is, nonetheless, to her former eternal
mate, to her love before her reincarnations, Mider. He appears to
her in the fifth section of the poem, a section which begins,
significantly, with a long description of the arrival of dawn. The
opening stanza of this description has a notable tonal unity:

> Hard by the swift-winged star, the moth-like moon
> Sheds golden dust on waves of day that ebb
> Into the deep beyond life's wan lagoon.
> The spider Night now spins his monstrous web,
> And spots the dark with many a pale cocoon
> Hung in his vaporous cave, whose phantoms creep
> In visions round the heavy brain of sleep. (26)

The web and the misty half-light create an atmosphere of eerie
promise in an unearthly world. But the description weakens in a
later stanza and descends to near-farce:

> Somewhere the snipe now taps his tiny drum;
> The moth goes fluttering upward from the heath;
> And where no lightest foot unmarked may come,
> The rabbit, tiptoe, plies his shiny teeth
> On luscious herbage; and with strident hum
> The yellow bees, blustering from flower to flower,
> Scatter from dew-filled cups a sparkling shower. (27)

Though there is triteness in the fluttering moth and the blustering bees, awkward inversion in "where no lightest foot unmarked may come," and selfconscious preciousness in the snipe tapping his tiny drum, the rabbit plying his shiny teeth, and the dew-filled cups of flowers scattering a shower, this stanza was particularly praised by a contemporary critic as revealing Cousins' "tender feeling for Nature."[10]

As dawn comes forth, Etain draws to a secluded place. A butterfly's wing brushes her cheek and stirs hidden memories in her of an "ancient ageless love" (28), and then Mider appears, all-knowing and all-loving. He clarifies the universal movements:

> And far from self thy feet have hither moved
> To the high purpose of the sacred fire
> That burns thine upward path through joy and pain,
> Through birth, through life, through death,
>   to me again. (30)

He comes from a domain beyond time, beyond change, beyond transmigration, a realm reached by inspiration, for which both of them are meant.

> Thine am I by the immemorial vow
> That made thee mine, beloved! eternally,
> When for a bride-price, on thy peerless brow
> I set a diadem beyond the worth
> Of all the crowns of all the queens of earth.
> . . .
> That land which gleams in the rapt poet's ken,
> Set in a sea that has no ebb or flow,
> Beyond the spear-cast of the dreams of men,
> Is mine, and from all changings far withdrawn
> There spreads the realm of Mider—and Etain. (31)

Mider opens to Etain her butterfly past wherein she was swallowed and reborn a daughter of earth; in addition, he explains that she is meant for immortal love, in lines in which James and Gretta Cousins' distress with the unaesthetic and degrading demands of humanity and nature in sex and regeneration are evident: "For thou were born for love whose windless sail/ Moves on great deeps beyond life's shallow range./ Love linked in flesh with failing flesh shall fail." (32) Mider's love, he explains, will brood and simmer until he again melds with Etain in a cosmic unity; in Mider's words,

> Till it at length come forth on perfect wing
> To brush with sweet eclipse the morning star,
> And in high heaven its utter rapture sing,
> Filling the universe with golden sound
> Of love immortal, measureless, unbound! (33)

Etain returns home with her extended vision of the infinite and how "small familiar things" are enlarged "with gleams from past the verge of sight," and made strange "with rumours of the infinite" (36), and she awaits the arrival of Mider. When Mider appears, he and Eochaid play chess on a jewelled board. To Eochaid's surprise, Mider wins, and then announces the stakes: Etain! Mider consoles the King with the line, "Thou in life's loss the Spirit's gain will find." (40) Mider's submission to the chess match for a prize he could merely have taken, Cousins viewed as symbolic of Mider's taking part in a lower nature, as Christ did when he became human.

There is a delay before Mider may claim his winnings, and in that delay Eochaid develops increasing insight that something important, inevitable, and just is being enacted. Still, he loves Etain, and does not want to part with her. The last part of the poem brings the inevitable day of the reunion of Mider and Etain, and the King's enlightened awareness and blessing. Mider appears, "a shining God/ From whose majestic presence swiftly spreads/ Peace not of earth." (46) The King now sees completely the divine plan:

> Now have I seen the shining hand of Him
> Who sifts the world for His divine desire;
> And gathers, and within His queen's wide rim
> Grinds all things meet for His transforming fire,
> And kneads them to a purpose far and dim;
> Who fashions all things to His growing plan,
> And breaks . . . and moulds . . . and breaks
>   the heart of man. (46)

The poem ends with a depiction of the unified Etain and Mider, the reunion symbolizing the return to the single benevolent point of origin of all earthly elements.

> A blinding fire falls from night's glimmering slope.
> Flame-like the twain meet on the rushy floor—
> And vanish. King and clansmen blindly grope

> Into cool air. Across the sky two swans
> Fly slowly toward the day that palely dawns. (46)

As in "The Marriage of Lir and Niav," the final union or culmination of love at the end of this poem is not as effective as the prelude.
The sublime is beyond Cousins' expression.

While the poem has occasional precious or conventional similes,
they do not seriously affect the poem's overall success, a success
primarily dependent upon the skillful control of the movement of
the narrative, with its rich and effective descriptive passages, such
as this stanza setting the scene for the arrival of Mider to claim
Etain.

> Then came a day when on the bare flag-stone
> The slow snail crawled; the chestnut's candle turned
> Downward as dead; the wolf-hound with a groan
> Gazed in King Eochaidh's eyes through eyes that burned
> Great threat; the spear-grass hither and thither blown
> Bent on the sand and traced its rings awry,
> And sun and moon slid down the sky. (44)

Sustained periods of delicate mood created by semi-ethereal imagery and by gracefully felicitous lines of soft sound and rhythm
add to the poem's merits.

The stanza Cousins evolves for this poem, forsaking the blank
verse and the Spenserian stanzas of the previous narratives, is a
pattern somewhat similar to the *rhyme royale*. Cousins sustains the
seven-line stanza throughout. It is difficult to overlook the seemingly deliberate numerical composition. The seven-section poem in
stanzas of seven lines, the seven seas, the seven sons, the seven
times seven leagues in the earlier narratives connote the magical
symbolism of the number seven.

The poem reveals further the variety of Cousins' technical
abilities, which he continuingly turns to an artistic synthesis of his
own interior vision. For, despite the ephemeral nature of his topic
and the temptation to explication, he moves the narrative steadily
without losing form, and with no needless digression. He said about
finding the legendary material of the poem,

I could not resist the temptation to another imaginative pilgrimage around
the inevitable cycle of life, particularly as the story, being psychological
rather than cosmic, took me nearer to the intimacies of the individual

human spirit in its fall and rise from allegiance to allegiance: nearer also to the exquisite constants of nature in which my own spirit found entrance to a life of beautiful love and of an ever-increasing love of the beautiful.[11]

But this was also to prove the seminal point for all his verse, for just as his point of view never wavered from the Theosophical, his approach never varied.

As in the former narratives, in "Etain," Cousins is chiefly concerned with the relationship between high spiritual values and the human realm; the remote spiritual past shapes the present and causes the future return to perfection. The circles of reincarnations are meant as mythological perceptions of cosmic truths, and all of life and nature as earthly manifestations of spiritual realities. The entities of the entire poem—the characters, the events, the descriptions—become symbolic representations of Cousins' own philosophy of the universe, based, he thought, upon an unspoiled Celtic imagination. His main interest in his narrative poems is the relationship and ultimate unity of the real and unreal. However limited and Theosophically doctrinaire his conception of Irish mythology, Cousins preferred to think of himself as being in the mainstream of poets, like Blake, Shelley, and AE, who saw time as a "masquerade of eternity" and believed that "visible life is nine-tenths lived in an invisible life."[12]

"Etain the Beloved" is one of Cousins' best poems, and is the best poetic explication of his philosophic point of view, with the poem's meaning clearly emerging from the text. Nonetheless, Cousins further elaborated the meaning in a monograph entitled *The Story of Etain: A Celtic Myth and an Interpretation*, reprinted from *Theosophy in Ireland*,[13] and in his volume dealing more generally with mythological significances, *The Wisdom of the West*, discussed previously. He neglects in this material, as in the poem, the outcome of Ailill, who is forsaken as Etain progresses to Mider, just as Dagda was left behind as Dana went on to perfect unity in "The Going Forth of Dana." Realities are overlooked as the ethereal realm evolves. Cousins does, in his discussion, focus on the implications of a Celtic belief in rebirth which is similar to the steps in the Vedantic progression in Indian philosophy.

In Cousins' longer poems of his Dublin years, myth provided a symbolic representation of a harmonious and benevolent union of the spiritual realm with the tangible earthly realm, a union centered on a single force of good. Such an assurance and such a philosophic goal had been sought by numerous Romantic writers in English and eluded some of them. The cycle of life that Gaelic myth suggested—from divine unity to human fragmentation to divine union again—provided a spiritual validity in human existence that countered the disturbing Victorian and contemporary scientific discoveries and evolutionary theories that troubled faith since the later nineteenth century.

Cousins, like Yeats and George Russell, central figures in the Irish Literary Renaissance, was attracted to Theosophy for the spiritual value it introduced into humanity. The Irish Renaissance, somewhat like Theosophy itself, is in a clear line of development from the Romantic movement and Victorian thought. As such, Theosophy and Theosophical thought are significant in the Irish Renaissance, and "Etain the Beloved" clarifies its import. Its Theosophical thesis also provides a basis for interpreting the frequent occurrence in Irish literature of reincarnation and metempsychosis, a fascination of James Joyce; and the numerous incidents focusing on the relativity of time, matter, and identity.

Cousins' attempts at narrative poems essentially stop at the end of his years in Dublin. They are, however, along with the plays, the bulk of his efforts there, though interspersed with short poems. His skill in developing and moving plot in a narrative developed quickly. His attempt to overlay philosophical significance on the events did not develop well until his writing of "Etain the Beloved." Before that, the Theosophical import was unclear. While the intrusion of Cousins' philosophy in "Etain" is no doubt for some readers a limitation on the poem, "Etain" is, nonetheless, his best sustained narrative, poetically speaking. Cousins' efforts in narrative and drama in Dublin drew him away from his primary poetic expression—the lyric.

II *Short Poems*

The approach and the dominant theme of Cousins' lyric utterances are suggested by the lines from "Etain the Beloved": "The mystery of small, familiar things/ Made great with gleams from past the verge of sight/ And strange with rumours of the infinite." (36) Just as in his longer mythological poems in which an elaborate myth was representative of the complicated workings of the divine on a cosmic scale, in the short poems Cousins' individual perceptions of "small, familiar things"—a tree in winter, a man behind a plough, a rook or a corncrake—provided insight into the continuing infusion of the heavenly in the natural workings of earth. These perceptions of the supernatural in the natural and in the material give to the shorter poems, regardless of the subject matter and form, a oneness of temperament and a consistency of vision which, once developed and clear in Cousins' mind, remained firmly uniform throughout the long span of his lyric writing. Restless questioning or uncertainty in the philosophical satisfactions and comforts he evolved never occurred in Cousins' short poems. Nor is there a pattern of periods of development, reflecting changing attitudes or outlooks. While Cousins' skill in technique and the refinement of expression improved and matured in his Dublin years, the same mental and artistic stamp was impressed on all the poems.

A. *The Developing Framework*

The earliest poem in which Cousins' lyric framework is clearly evident is the title poem of *The Voice of One* (1900). In these lines, the persona Cousins is to use and develop throughout the lyrics emerges as one aspiring towards and responding to the divine.

> I am the voice of one who cries:
> Lo! here I cannot stop or stay.
> I am not good, I am not wise,
> I only follow far away;
>
> And, seeing not, I yearn for sight
> To read the heart of praise or blame,
> To catch the beam within the light,
> And feel the fire behind the flame;
>
> . . .
> And know that thing for which I seek
> With frustrate fingers blind and dead;
> And turn Truth's never-ceasing wheel,
> And from its distaff weave my thread.[14]

In later life, Cousins felt that in these lines he found clear expression of his "desire for immediate (not mediate) intercourse with what I would call the super-phenomenal world rather than the noumenal world in its etymological sense of an unknown and unknowable something beyond the phenomenal."[15] And indeed the simplicity of expression yields unusual clarity to that elusive desire. The seeking of this kind is reminiscent of the Tennysonian desire to see beyond the veil separating the spirit realm from the earthly reality, a frequent desire in Victorian writers. While Cousins was much influenced by Romantic and Victorian English verse, he is more immediately an Irish poet and a product of the Irish Revival, with its search for spiritual idealism. Throughout his decades in India and in spite of his feeling spiritually at home there, Cousins continued to define himself specifically as a Celt with a Celtic imagination.[16] His particular spiritual odyssey was prompted by the lure of the eternal as envisioned in Celtic myth; the poet is enticed by a realm of immortals, a land of dreams and heroes. The enticement in Cousins follows in tone the Romantic lyricism of the early verse of Yeats. Reminiscent of Yeats' "The Stolen Child," some representative Cousins lines read,

> *Shoheen, sho-lo:*
> Hark, the Bell-branch ringing.
> *Shoheen, sho-lo:*
> Dannans from the hills are singing:
> *"Time is old, and earth is gray,—*
> *Come, ye weary ones, away,*
> *Where, with white, untroubled brows*
> *The Immortals dream and drowse,*
> *And the streams of quiet flow."*[17]

The Dannans are invisible ones "who, in Ireland, call men away from the world of sense to the inner world of spiritual reality," frequently by ringing a branch of bells (26). As with much of the verse of the Revival, there is here a turning to a shadowy, but eternal realm embodied in the figures of Celtic mythology.

Cousins' desire for "the super-phenomenal world" finds its fulfillment in the Theosophical view he came to in his Dublin years; the material and the natural are merely manifestations of the spirit. Hence, he does not turn from, but embraces, the material and unites it with the spiritual, as a manifestation of the spiritual. And Cousins sees himself, as he sees all humans, as part of the eternal spiritual; thus the voice in the title poem of *The Quest* in 1906 is that of the poet moving from the human to the cosmic. The details of the quest are like those in Shelley's "Hymn to Intellectual Beauty." Cousins' lines are:

> They said: "She dwelleth in some place apart,
>   Immortal Truth, within whose eyes
>   Who looks may find the secret of the skies
> And healing for life's smart."
>
> I sought Her in loud caverns underground,—
>   On heights where lightnings flashed and fell;
>   I scaled high Heaven; I stormed the gates of Hell,
> But Her I never found,
>
> Till thro' the tumults of my Quest I caught
>   A whisper: "Here, within thy heart,
>   I dwell, for I am thou: behold, thou art
> The Seeker—and the Sought."[18]

The same idea is stated by an inner Voice in the sestet of the sonnet, "Vision" (1907), in *The Awakening*. Once again, the poet moves within the poem from ignorance to knowledge in a dynamic encounter with himself. And, as in *The Quest*, the complexity of persona reflects the poet's world view, for he is both the speaker and the listener.

>   . . . "Arise!
> Wisdom is wisdom only to the wise:
> Thou are thyself the Royal thou hast crowned:
> In Beauty thine own beauty thou hast found,
> And thou hast looked on God with God's own eyes."[19]

With this view, Cousins can say of himself,

> Beyond the bounds of death and birth
> I move, unmindful, unafraid:
> I am the God, and I the Earth,
> And life and death myself have made.[20]

This consciously-held philosophical view, derived partially from his individual reading of Celtic myth, has led some to call Cousins a mystic, a loose, though not infrequent, use of the term. His intellectual and philosophically-held view of the universe, no matter what its implications of immanent (or, for that matter, transcendent) mysticism, does not qualify Cousins as a true mystic who claims a fully-united absorption into the One. Cousins' belief that he is a manifestation of the ultimate spirit does not, *per se*, dissolve that manifestation into the total ultimate spirit with full awareness of all manifestations and all knowing that is held to be the true mystical experience. Cousins is more precisely a Theosophical, rather than a mystical, poet who consistently and comprehensively saw evidence for his Theosophical beliefs in the range of "familiar things" on earth. To survey Cousins' short poems, then, it is helpful to discuss the familiar subjects that appear frequently in his lyrics.

B. *Subject Matter: Nature*

As could be expected with Cousins' Romantic vision and his Theosophy, nature was a primary incitement to verse. Throughout his life, he was a keen observer of nature, whose small details he could always place in his cosmic scheme. Appropriately, birds were frequent subjects, often representing Cousins' yearning for and identification with a freedom of spirit. Cousins' earlier poem, "The Corncrake," which sometimes appears in anthologies of Irish verse, reveals his experimentation within the lyric and suggests, at the end, the bird's awareness of eternity.

> I heard him faintly, far away,
>   (*Break! Break!—Break! Break!*)
> Calling to the dawn of day,
>   "Break! Break!"
>
> I heard him in the yellow morn
>   (*Shake! Shake!—Shake! Shake!*)
> Shouting thro' the rustling corn,
>   "Shake! Shake!"
>
> I heard him near where one lay dead
>   (*Ache! Ache!*)
> Crying among poppies red,
>   "Ache! Ache!—Ache! Ache!"
>
> And where a solemn yew-tree waves
>   (*Wake! Wake!*)
> All night he shouts among the graves,
>   "Wake! Wake!—Wake! Wake!"[21]

The use of the bird's "talk" and the cleverness of the reversal of the line length of the second and fourth lines in the last two stanzas hint at a playfulness that seems at odds with the traditional images of death suggested by the yews and the red poppies, but prepare for the apparently confident command of the corncrake, with its instinctive, natural awareness that the dead awake.

As images of freedom and awareness, birds inspire and teach Cousins, as did the skylark for Shelley. In the poem, "Three White Eagles,"[22] the three eagles suggest a lesson in the Trinity. In "Flight," reflecting its Indian setting, a blue bird images Cousins' spirit. The poem begins with a request.

> Blue bird on the mango bough!
> Teach me how
> I may spread my wings like you
> In the blue;
> For I think I too can fly
> If I only try.
> *Why?* you question, *Why?*
> I shall tell you why.

Cousins then describes the flight of his spirit, the short lines suggesting the freedom of release.

> Sometimes in the quiet night
> Comes a light
> In the middle of my head;
> Then I spread
> Arms to left and right wing-wise,
> Slowly, slowly rise
> From the ground
> Without a sound;
> Hang a dizzy foot or so,
> Then let go
> And sail away
> Like a flake of day
> Blown across the wondering dark
> Till my spark
> Lengthens, flickers into tails,
> Shakes and fails,
> And I waken with a start
> At my heart!
> And as now in sunset rays
> On you I gaze and gaze and gaze,
> I begin to think

> I feel the round world sink;
> Yes, I leave the ground, I rise
> Through my dazzled eyes
> To become a part of you,
> Of the very jumping heart of you,
> The fearless outward spring of you,
> The spread glad wing of you!
> Bird, O bird! that now
> Leaves the mango bough,
> See me, see me panting at your side
> Swimming down the swirling flashing sunset tide!

The experience of identification with the bird has not only inspired, but enlightened Cousins.

> . . . I seem
> In my mind to find the print
> Of a hint
> Of a deep infolded Power
> That shall flower
> Not alone to flight
> At your cloudy height,
> But along a singing way
> Through and past the cage of clay;
> Yea a Power that yet will spread
> Rainbow wings of Godlihead,
> When the inner has come out . . .
> When we leave control
> With the Soul . . . (185 - 87)

The conventional metaphors and the intrusive internal and regular rhyme do not contribute positively to the poem, but its message of man's organic involvement with nature is clear. Nature draws out the soul of man for its transcendent awareness of the all-pervasive cosmic spirit.

Cousins is also often attracted to other elements of nature that have to do with the sky or are not held to earth. "Above the Rainbow," like "Flight," has lyrically exultant moments, here generated by a rainbow. Cousins stands "on a Himalayan height/ Watching the shower and the sunlight march," and sees a rainbow lift its "spectral lines." "Above, in heavenly gardens, shines/ The eternal snow-flowers' waxen bloom." Cousins' spirit responds:

> I take the challenge of the bird
> Exulting past the rainbow's rise:
> Lightly upon the spirit's word
> I leave the earth and seek the skies;
>
> I spread my pinions on the blast,
> Casting the cage of date and name,
> Above the hint of waters past,
> Beyond the threat of future flame. (301)

The regularity of the iambic tetrameter, the vocabulary and the alliteration weigh down the poem's intended soaring. Here, as in "Flight," a bird symbolizes the soaring spirit, a spirit that in melding with an oversoul leaves behind its individual identity—"Casting the cage of date and name"—in time and matter. As part of the oversoul, it recognizes its existence before Genesis or the Flood, "Above the hint of waters past," and beyond the end of the world, "Beyond the threat of future flame." The mystery of a "small, familiar" thing—a bird or a rainbow—has been invested with "rumours of the infinite" and intimations of immortality.

A pair of poems treating the rain—"Before Rain" and "Song After Rain"—have particular interest. While spiritual solace coming from nature is frequent in Cousins, as in "Flight" and "Above the Rainbow," the absence of and need for spiritual solace rarely gets direct attention. The poem, "Before Rain," focuses on the intensity of the need. The rain symbolizes the spiritual solace and calm it brings in "Song After Rain."

"Before Rain," because of its unique tone of near desperation for Cousins, its near throbbing vocabulary, and its skillful use of the scene to symbolize the interior, gasping, spiritual thirst merits full quotation.

> All day a heart pulsed in the brooding sky.
> All day a brain beat out a thought.
> And heart and brain in single purpose wrought
> So sharp an agony,
> That one whom life had taught
> To read sky-portents with unclouded sight,
> Knew that, ere fall of night,
> Someone in heaven or on the earth must cry.
>
> All that, towards which, through eyes that searched
>   and burned,

A thousand thousand days aspired;
All that long sleepless nights had long desired;
All guerdon sought or scorned;
All that was vision-fired
By holy things most passionately hoped
When dream-doors shut or oped,
Mixed now, and moved, and to heart-breaking yearned.

Now on the earth a burden trails along.
All things are silent that should speak.
The very parrots pass without a shriek.
The rooks in conclave throng.
The mina's tail hangs meek.
A dumb dropped tree its waiting shadow shakes
Over a heart that aches
For birth into its heritage of song.

At last! at last! to those made weather-wise
Flashes the sign that all fulfils.
Hark! the old lion, thunder, through the hills
Growls with swift glaring eyes.
Now! past our palsied wills,
Flame, with its lancing pennants, thrilling drums,
Unto deliverance comes
With a great shout of birth that shakes the skies!

Then comes the rain!—a drop; a coin as wage
For waiting: then the deepening shower.
Earth is scrawled o'er with flowing songs an hour.
O heart! be thou a page
Vocal with so great power!
So shall we, with a word's victorious helm,
Emancipate a realm,
And in a line immortalise an age! (270 - 71)

The unusual strength of the vocabulary is a rarity for Cousins, who is more usually given to idyllic, inspiring, and ethereal descriptions. The implication is strong that Cousins did at some time experience a period of spiritual discomfort, of the withdrawal of the spiritual solace that elsewhere in his poetry he readily found everywhere. In this poem, the description of the scene involves the whole earth, along with Cousins, in a desperate and painful yearning, as evidenced in the "brooding sky" that mirrors the "sharp agony of the heart and brain" and the "cry of someone in heaven or on earth."

The aching pain of the "searching, burning" eyes is also prolonged, "a thousand thousand days and long sleepless nights" of "heart-breaking yearning," until the rain comes. Even the rain, representative of spiritual balm, is announced in uniquely strong words for Cousins. A thunderstorm, it comes as a lion with growls and glaring eyes. There is "flame and flashes" and "shout that shakes the skies." The intensity of the need and the pain of the spiritual desert, subject matter, elsewhere absent in Cousins, finds its expression in natural imagery expressed with a new tone and vocabulary for Cousins. But the need finds its fulfillment in the "deepening shower that scrawls flowing songs across the earth."

"Song After Rain" treats of the rejoicing comfort from the spiritual rain that has slaked the earth. The soft tones of comfort in spiritual awareness drawn from and symbolized by the rain are more typically present, as all of earth feels the bliss.

> Oh! love has fallen as a shower;
> And out of hidden nurseries
> In breaking buds and swinging trees,
> At call of that forth-bidding power,
> From secret cradles under leaves,
> And under cool palmyra eaves,
> Life casts her chrysalis, and springs
> To dance where dancing sunlight goes,
> And turn the heart's flower-bordered rows
> From prim acceptance of repose
> To moth-made revelry of wings!
>
> Oh! love has fallen as a shower;
> And through the palpitating blue
> The shrieking circling swallow-crew
> Build up a high invisible tower
> With madcap magic of design
> Sketched in grey-lightning curve and line;
> Then break, and cry in mimic woe
> For very access of delight,
> And fill the eye with chase and flight
> Of swirling leaves bewildered quite
> When the great winds contrarious blow!
>
> Oh! love has fallen as a shower;
> And the hibiscus of the heart,
> That bled within the bud apart,

> Unfolds its hanging scarlet flower;
> And all its fervent hope distils
> Into a crystal drop that thrills
> With urgent bliss upon its tongue.
> Heart-full of rainbow speech it aches;
> In joy of near fulfilment shakes,
> And on the verge of utterance breaks
> In one great tear for song unsung! (272 - 73)

The concealed spirit emerges from the "hidden nurseries" and "secret cradles" as the buds open, the trees sway in wafting currents of air, and life dances as does the sunlight. Cousins, like earth, is brought again to be part of a vibrant spiritual presence. There is a possible temptation to read this poem as replete with sexual imagery. The first line of each of the three stanzas—"Oh! love has fallen as a shower"—introduces the possibility with its mention of love. The first stanza tells of the emergence of the secret and the hidden, and leads into the "palpitating blue" and the "building up of a high tower" in the second stanza, which then moves to the "very access of delight." Stanza three with its "unfolding of the hanging scarlet flower" and the "crystal drop that thrills" brings this reading to its orgasmic completion. But such a reading is probably a perversion of Cousins' conscious intentions, since we do know that he and his wife found physical sex unartistic and beneath human dignity. Such thinking does not, however, uniformly suppress sexual desire.

The only other poem in which Cousins uses a natural scene to depict the absence of spiritual infusion is "The First Wind." Quite different from "Before Rain," the description is of the "vast quiet at the first of things," at the time of creation.

> So stood the trees in that primeval trance.
> No zephyr gave the lilt for leafy dance,
> Or set the tune to shake the moony night
> To glittering ecstasies of leaf and light.
> Only great solitude was round their feet.

The first wind symbolizes the infusion of the divine.

> In buried rootlet and frustrated seed
> Moved from aeonian sleep the Powers of air
> At their first breath each leaf grew whisperer;

> And through the trees deep agitation went
> As from His hand . . .

The forest is then brought into a "revelling song" as

> Joy that sighed down until the blissful trees
> Purred to the silken handstroke of the breeze. (263 - 65)

While the poem describes the absence and the arrival of divine solace as does the pair of rain poems above, the poem does not spell out any urgent pain of yearning as does "Before Rain." The arrival of the spirit, while expressed with a different metaphor of nature, is similar in tone to "Song After Rain."

Another sky-conscious image—like birds, rainbows, rain, wind—that Cousins uses with success is the sunset. In "Invitation at Sunset," Cousins effectively communicates the spiritual peace and broad wisdom that he found in nature. Clear in its presentation of his view of nature, it is a high point in his nature verse.

> Come where the coriander its aromatic breath
> Exhales as a loosened spirit that seeks not the
>   boon of rest;
> Where, high in the tamarind, mews like a kitten the
>   bird of death,
> Its eye on the chittering weaver-bird that shrinks
>   its vest.
>
> Holy the daylight was. As holy shall be the dark.
> Holy the place and the moment where life to life
>   now calls.
> Holy the shrine-topped kondas that east- and westward
>   mark
> The Day-God's myriad births and myriad burials.
>
> Shall we hold that the day's fulfillment is all on
>   the forehead bowed
> Of Light, by Darkness dethroned and humbled in
>   red retreat?
> Nay, look you! above the standards of Night a
>   crimson cloud
> Floats as a flag from a bastion denying the
>   Day's defeat.
>
> A million days . . . and a million . . . and the end

> thereof who knows?
> What will be, will be. What is, our lifted hands
>   acclaim.
> Lost not in the sweet and splendid sadness of how
>   day goes,
> We lost not the joy of the triumph and wonder of how
>   it came. (447 - 48)

The lushness of the aromatic setting, the slow-moving long lines, and the repeated declaration of the holiness of earth mix with the hints of sadness of death and burial to make the poem a melancholy and moving assertion of faith and acceptance of life as it moves toward the inevitable spiritual apotheosis. For Cousins, "the joy of the triumph and wonder of how it came" is secure.

Cousins also uses numerous images from nature that are other than those that are above the earth. Frequent among these are streams and mountains. In "The Brook Sings," the brook itself speaks, calling to those who seek "quiet bliss" and "sanctifying solitude," and the brook clarifies that its "radiant moments glow/ Only in my seaward flow." Cousins then explains the metaphor of the brook's message.

> Thus the brook: and as it sings
> Snatches from the theme of things
> Meaning mounts from hidden springs,
> Bearing towards a hidden sea
> Fragments of the mystery
> Mixed in man and brook and tree. (258 - 62)

The numerous streams and waterways moving towards the sea of eternity are an apt and useful, if conventional, metaphor for Cousins' Theosophical purport.

Mountains are weightier images for Cousins than those discussed above, but they appear often, as in "At the Twelve Bens, Connemara"[23] and in "How the Mountains Came to Be."[24] Typical of Cousins' use of the mountain image are these lines from "Morning Worship."

> Something my wakening soul has stirred!
>
> . . .
>
> Look up! See, tipped with rose,
> White on the sky's blue lake, the vast
> Himalayan lotus blows!

> O perfect Beauty's loftiest mood!
> O Peace that shall endure!
> O high unsullied Solitude!
> O purity most pure! (302)

Mountains, with their strength, permanence, and nobility are representative evidence of the strength, permanence, and nobility of the divine in nature, and stir Cousins to heights of spiritual awareness, as do the less awesome elements of nature.

In his Romantic attention to nature, Cousins does not omit rustic scenes, including those of humans living close to and in harmony with nature. "A Flail Song" and "A Song of Sowing and Reaping" idealize rural tasks, as does "Behind the Plough," whose last lines invest the task with a supernatural metaphor:

> I follow the feet of the Horses
> That drag the Morning Star,
> To search in the spoils of the furrow,
> Where God the Ploughman ploughs.[26]

And no doubt taking his inspiration from Robert Burns, an early interest of his, Cousins has a "Talk to a Field-Mouse" in which he explains his kinship with the mouse as part of the cosmic divine.

> Himself in us He has immured:
> We are not shades of Him, but He! (154)

As in the rest of Cousins' verse, the "smallest things" hold "rumours of the infinite."

Nature, then, was a rich and primary vein for Cousins' observation of the presence of the supernatural he felt so strongly. In it, he always found and praised the Spirit; indeed, his praise of nature is praise of the Spirit. For him they are one and the same. His nature verse, as stated in "The Theme," is a hymn to God.

> I sing of waters, winds and trees.—
> But no! I do not sing of these.
> One theme alone my Daemon sings:—
> The Spirit mixed in mortal things.
> She sings no passing wind or tree:
> She sings their haunting mystery. (278)

C.   *Subject Matter: Ireland*

It was in the mode of the Irish Literary Revival for Ireland's earth
to be raised to holy sod. Cousins, with his view of nature, was in the
main current of the Revival as he observed and responded to things
Irish. As in the work of many of his contemporary writers, Cousins'
verse frequently uses or develops from a sense of a specific place in
Ireland, as seen in "At the Twelve Bens, Connemara":

> With gorgeous pageantry of light and cloud,
> The mighty Bens this morn above me rose.
> Clothing their agony of ancient throes
> In awful majesty, aloof and proud;
> Like elder gods to whom all wisdom bowed,
> Who, passed thro' sweetening flame and cleansing snows,
> Now fill the thrones of infinite repose,
> To utmost calm and contemplation vowed.
>
> O solemn power of Beauty that is born
> Of vast calamity and hoary time!
> Spirit, whose smile transfigures ruining fate!
> Be hers, whose eyes are weary for the morn;
> Be mine, to fill her ear with hope's glad chime:
> *Peace! my beloved, a little longer wait.*[27]

The mighty mountains caught in the light of morning draw
Cousins' attention and suggest the strength of calm repose which
fills the Connemara scene, which, in turn suggests the awesome
spirit and eternal beauty which are present in and bless these holy
hills.

Other poems about Ireland, while in the same calm tone, deal
more abstractly with the spirit of the nation, as seen in "To Ireland—I":

> God willed of old to lift thine ancient Name,
> That thou, thro' suffering made most wise, most pure,
> Shouldst bear before all men the Soul's white lure,
> And lead them to and thro' the purging flame.
> But, lest thine eager feet should foil the aim
> Of Time's slow builders, building strong and sure,
> He mingled with thy fire, that shall endure,
> Somewhat of earth, for shackle, not for shame.

> Thou are not wholly earth, nor all divine;
> And tho' rude hands of sons undutiful
> Build in the clay, and soil thy royal dress,
> Mother of deathless kings! let joy be thine!
> Thou still hast beauty for the beautiful,
> And proud, glad lovers for thy loveliness.[28]

The lines call up Ireland's ancient heritage and name; the centuries of suffering are cited; and the present "rude hands of sons undutiful" (the English?) are referred to. But Ireland's pure, white Soul endures, made wise through suffering—a Soul that is to be born before all men and to lead them. Later, George Russell was to claim this spiritual leadership for Ireland in his *National Being*, as was Yeats in a particularly poetic way, in "The Statues" and "Under Ben Bulben." Also notable is the distinctively Irish dual perception. Ireland is both natural and supernatural: "Thou art not wholly earth, nor all divine," but for Cousins Ireland is a bit of each. While the poem is not a particularly political poem, the nationalistic optimism and the imaginative idealism in the 1908 poem are representative of that which inspired the band of poets and school teachers who led the 1916 Easter Rebellion in Dublin.

While Cousins is poetically and generally silent about the troubles and bloodshed in Ireland in 1916 and the years following, having been settled in India by this time, the English-Irish treaty of 1921, itself the cause of considerable Irish strife, did bring forth a poem, "To Ireland, Before the Treaty of December, 1921," acknowledging his brooding concern and continuing love for his country:

> Not the loud songs of joyful ease
> I give, as once on morning's wing;
> But, for your night of agonies,
> I give dark songs I cannot sing.
>
> Take them, beloved! and, deeper, far
> Than moods that wear a transient name,
> Take love whose wordless poems are
> The throbbing silence round a flame;
>
> Love that my veins with passion thrids,
> Kindling your candles in my eyes,
> And from my heart's red censer bids
> Perpetual worship rise. (285)

The implication is that though Ireland is in a dark period, a "night of agonies," that the suffering is transient and that Ireland is part of the permanent flame; Cousins adds his love to "perpetual worship" that Ireland receives.

His return visit to Ireland in 1925, with its disappointing meeting with Yeats and George Russell, brought forth a commonplace poem, "Ireland After Ten Years," written at Rosses in Sligo. The poem opens with a greeting to Ireland: "Land of my birth! again I greet/ Thy grey-wing sky, green earth, sweet air;"—and then, recalling the recent years of Irish troubles, laments the "long red saga's wave" which "beyond thy dream's edge sinks from view." As the poem moves to its positive conclusion, Cousins asks that the Irish "brave the splendid hazard of the New" while drinking from the Irish "ancient, wise, enchanted springs" so that Ireland's Last will be its First—"A glory sought by saints and kings" (285 - 86). For Cousins, Ireland's spirit was eternal and its spiritual leadership inevitable.

A more significant poem, "To Ireland," was written several years later in India, and is a poetic acknowledgment of Cousins' allegiance to Ireland, an allegiance "deeper," he said, "than nativity": "Unto my heart's wild seaway strife/ . . . You were to me the door of life,/ But life grew larger than its door." The poem nostalgically calls up a series of specific past delights of Ireland. Among them are:

> I loved your paths, for on them dawned
> The vision of the Hidden Way
> Through passion to a tryst beyond
> The transient liaison of clay.
>
> I loved your toil, when seed was laid,
> Or flail-men parted grain and husk.
> I loved the joy of man and maid
> Dancing at Ventry in the dusk.
>
> I loved your moods of gold and grey;
> That hour when, to the heart's delight,
> The ebbing deluge of the day
> Left quivering drops on boughs of night.

Cousins also recalls inspiring locations in Ireland:

> I know a legend-haunted place

> Where I can wander night or day
> With quick or dead, the ancient race
> Of comrades on the upward Way;
>
> Poets who heard a distant drum
> That rallied visions to their eyes
> Of holy Ireland free; and some
> Who gladly fell that She might rise.
>
> And in and out through these will go
> The flicker of the flame-faced kings
> Who touch men's hearts with heavenly glow
> And give their thoughts the lift of wings.
>
> These unto me their hands will reach
> Over the archway of the sun,
> Speaking the single spirit-speech
> From heights where East and West are one.
>
> Before my blinding morning breaks
> I shall step out behind a star
> And seek the quiet haunted lakes
> And hills where my De Dananns are. (359 - 60)

The attention to the moods of Irish scenery, and to the country activities, remains consistent, as does the recall of the holiness of Ireland and its ancient legends and Cousins' acknowledgment that his Irish visions have led him to that place "where East and West are one," and will ultimately lead him to the spiritual eternity where the Irish gods, the De Dananns, are.

Celtic mythology, which had been the main substance of his narrative poems written in Ireland, surfaced, as might be expected, in short poems also. Appropriately, Cousins wrote a poem about Niamh, the Irish goddess who took the legendary Oisin to the Land of the Forever Young. In this sonnet, "The Coming of Niamh," Niamh lures the speaker, apparently Cousins, "past the verge of sight."

> Softly, as comes a wind across the sea
> That thrills the waves to music on the beach,
> And stirs the trees to whisperings each to each,
> And bids the birds pipe low sweet song of glee;

> So, like a summer morning, came to me
> My Queen, my Niamh; and her gentle speech
> Spake regal lineage longer than the reach
> Of memory, older than the thrones that be.
> And thro' the tumults that around me rise,
> She speaks of hidden and tremendous things—
> Grails yet unwon, and Quests that never cease;
> And calls me forth to where, with quenchless eyes,
> She with the deathless dwells, and folds her wings
> Enthroned in vast, unutterable Peace.[29]

Even after Cousins had been in India for several years, his muse, he said, remained Celtic. "The Celtic Gods were still in their heaven, which was not beyond the stars, even if nothing was quite right with the world for the purposes of a sensitive poet."[30] While the Niamh poem above was written in Dublin, Irish mythology recurred in India as a subject for short poems. Notable are "The Testing of Finn" (361), touching on Finn Mc Cumhail, the bardic hero; and "The Oracle," dealing once more with the Celtic gods Dagda and Dana. In "The Oracle," the poet has

> died from feet to head;
> Then floated free to climb
> Beyond long clouds of dread
> Into a place that had
> The sun and moon for doors.

The enlightenment of the poet, which recalls in the telling the poet's enlightenment in Keats' "Fall of Hyperion," occurs when the poet meets a goddess of the Irish pantheon, who unseals his sight, telling him that those "Who deem the Gods are dead,/ Or born of haunted brain/ Out of primeval dread,/ Have their own Godhead slain." But to the newly-arrived poet, she says,

> O you whose feet have climbed
> Our hidden citadel!
> Time's eye on the untimed,
> Behold, remember, tell
> How they who bravely win
> High aspiration's wings
> Shall reach our heaven within
> Far or familiar things.

She assigns the poet his task, to rekindle in the world awareness of
the existence of the Powers. And then, the poet awakens,

> Reborn from head to feet,
> Out of a place that has
> Birth, death, for swinging doors;
> Where Shapes ancestral pass
> Along star-stippled floors,
> Weaving in holy dance
> From threads of night and morn
> The cradling circumstance
> Of worlds that will be born. (419 - 23)

In this dream vision, finished in India in 1934, Cousins' Celtic imagination and his Theosophical optimism remained secure. The
poem also suggests Cousins' continued reading of Romantic poets,
in this instance Keats, and his lasting sympathy with their desire for
an apocalyptic vision. The poem also evidences the lasting place
that Ireland retained as a central subject matter for Cousins, even
after so many long years of self-imposed exile.

D.   *Subject Matter: India and Places on Travels*

The lyric responses to India during Cousins' four decades there
are numerous. Most of these are essentially nature poems depicting
the expansive lushness of that subcontinent, a lushness that was a
fertile and fitting subject for Cousins' tremulous appreciation and
soothingly elevating lines, as seen in the lines from "Invitation at
Sunset," cited previously in discussion of Cousins' use of
nature—"Come where the coriander its aromatic breath/ Exhales as
a loosened spirit that seeks not the boon of rest," etc. Some are occasional poems moved by events of personal note to Cousins in India, such as, "Clay, to Commemorate a Student-sculptor's First
Model," and "Installation Ode: For the First Woman Magistrate in
India" (Gretta Cousins, installed in 1923). It is fitting that Cousins
was inspired to verse by that beautiful architectural masterpiece,
the Taj Mahal. His poem of that name opens with one of Cousins'
pointed paradoxes:

> What love exhaled what beauty! What desire
> Broke whitely past the flesh, and in dumb stone
> Found silence louder than the heart's wild tone

That for vast sorrow raised this moonlit pyre!
. . .
Vain! vain! His grief for us to bliss has grown
Through beauty's quenchless and preserving fire.

Canst Thou not leave us to our little ends,
Allah? nor our dear purposes annoy
With something deeper than the eye can see,
As here, where, more than stricken love intends,
Sorrow is throned on everlasting joy,
And death is crowned with immortality.

In the next section of the poem, Cousins commemorates the builders and workers of the Taj, who, though now lost and forgotten, have an enduring monument in this "House of Life"; and asks of Allah for himself, as a worker in life, "oblivion in Thy shining Face," for Allah alone remains. In a similar progress from earthly reality to ethereal permanence, the next part of the poem describes the Taj and its surroundings coming to life at sunrise, with particular focus on the sounds of life as they rise and echo and murmur in the dome, becoming a "celestial sound." Another plea to Allah asks for the ability to hear the "authentic Voice," the "Infinite low-murmuring" near earth. The poem then ends, with a concluding entreaty to Allah that human eyes be open to the intangible realities, in Theosophical fashion.

Open our eyes, and unto them display,
Allah! the hidden Taj that through our strife
Invisibly we build with passion's fire
And thought's high sculpturing. Grant us each day
Beautiful burial, sweet death in life,
And peace at last beside the heart's desire! (193 - 95)

While Cousins here treats of a work of man—the Taj—rather than a work of nature, the insight and the movement of the poem are the same, penetrating to the spiritual reality inherent in all things. The other poems in India are predictable in their treatment of the landscape and in their thematic spirituality.

The verse from Cousins' year in Japan is generally weak, some of it recalling, in its poor rhyme and shorter line, some of the weak early verse, like "A Spring Rondel by a Starling." The opening of "Gladiolus, in an Oriental Garden," reveals these poetic lapses:

> In my gardening sauntering solus
> Came I on a gladiolus;
> But before I bent my knee
> Something strange occurred to me!
>
> What had been a flower now glowed a
> Crimson-lanterned peaked pagoda,
> Sacred to the More-than-man
> In the islands of Japan. (274)

The strain in thought, rhyme, and vocabulary to turn a moment in Japan into a Theosophical enlightenment is evident.

In Hawaii, a volcano moves Cousins to verse, the poem "Morning Song in Hawaii," which, after an opening stanza of description, moves to the inevitable insight of the volcano's deeper essence:

> Oh! more than thanks of flower and tree
> She hath from opened eyes that see
> In falling rain, in seas that smile
> Around this paradisal isle,
> And in the spent volcano's cone,
> A deeper Being than their own,
> Which rounds to beauty the uncouth
> Cicatrix of a fiery youth,
> And changes to a mood of mirth
> The ancient agonies of earth! (340 - 41)

Cousins' sojourn in Europe in 1932 and 1933 produced a series of "European Sonnets," and his stay in Capri resulted in a group of "Capri Sonnets and Songs." These sonnets tend to contain his general Theosophical themes, though a few are descriptive of a specific scene. The rigidity and containment of the sonnet form makes Cousins' lyric flights more tersely effective. Of particular interest is one of the European sonnets in which he turns to the pageantry enacted in the commemoration of the Feast of Epiphany as subject matter for his call to the oneness of spirit. Implied are Cousins' feelings of the limitations in Christianity as he watches the religious procession.

> Now they have passed beyond their Christmas feast;
> And, fleshly-willed, resume their fleshly care
> That mocks the Message and the Messenger;
> And turn to you, O Wise Men from the East!

> They hear the voice of parson and of priest
> Telling of gold and frankincense and myrrh;
> And think your gifts no richer gifts declare,
> And you and them a tale that long has ceased.
> Oh wisdom, Aspiration, Purity
> Bring once again for One who newly comes,
> And give to Earth a new Epiphany.
> For in the scroll of creature-martyrdoms
> Perpetual Good Friday had sufficed—
> The ceaseless crucifixion of the Christ! (394 - 95)

A tone of distance and disdain, not particularly fitting for one who believed that spiritual truth was to be found in all religions, is evident in Cousins' obvious detachment from the *they* of the poem. The scorn of human physicality in the Christians, revealed by Cousins' repetition of "fleshly care" and "fleshly-willed," is stated more directly by the statement that the celebrants "mock" Christ and his message, and is reinforced by the supposed materialism represented by gold, frankincense, and myrrh. The implication of the conclusion, with its plea for another epiphany, another divine revelation, is that if these Christians followed the path of Cousins' enlightenment, the continued ridicule of Christ's spiritual message would cease. The poem is one of the few evidences of a lack of kindness or broadmindedness in Cousins, though it is not a rare evidence of his egotism.

E.   *Subject Matter: Friendship and Love*

Uppermost in Cousins' Theosophy was the spiritual bond linking human beings. It is evident in his autobiography that he lived his belief in seeking out and in offering warm friendship to numerous people throughout the world. The names of some of these friends show up in Cousins' occasional verse, which, in most instances, fades into insignificance. Worthy of mention, however, are two poems about friends of Cousins, in both instances friends of some fame. In Ireland, Francis Sheehy-Skeffington, a friend and associate of Cousins in his publishing *The Pioneer* and in the suffragette movement, was, as Cousins said, "the first sacrificial victim in the Irish struggle at Easter, 1916. He was shot without trial though he was trying to restrain the populace from disorder when arrested." Cousins commemorated the event, and the friendship, in the poem, "In Memory of Francis Sheehy-Skeffington" (165 - 66).

Among the satisfactions that India brought to Cousins was a continuing friendship with Tagore. "To Rabindranath Tagore" reflects Cousins' warm affection for that superior Indian poet. The dedication of Cousins' 1922 volume of verse, *Surya Gita: Sun Songs for Rabindranath Tagore,* is evidence of the strength of the attachment. But "To Rabindranath Tagore" speaks directly of the admiration and affection of Cousins, as seen in these concluding stanzas:

> Yet, since a sacramental hand
> May sanctify the humblest weed,
> I lift my love's transforming wand
> And give intention for the deed;
> With one deep wish that, till the set
> Of sun across your song's wide sea,
> Our backs may bend with growing debt
> For your pure golden poetry! (203)

But it is his wife Gretta who is the primary subject for Cousins' affection and love in verse. Generally, the focus is on the spiritual bond of love. It can be presumed that Cousins was in agreement with Gretta's stated distaste for physical union and sexual intercourse as being beneath human dignity. The spiritual union of male and female, as Cousins had interpreted Celtic mythology, was a step toward the ultimate unity of all things. Hence, the closing lines of "Love's Heresy":

> For I have seen how life in twain has rent
> —To find completion more completely whole
> Beyond the achievement of the separate soul—
> The spirit's orient and occident.
> And I have hope, that, for my sight's reward,
> Our here disjoined unperfect hearts may reach
> Through daily song's antiphoned accord,
> One high, harmonious, consecrated speech;
> And, when our love goes silent at its brim,
> We may present one perfect heart to Him. (407)

Love, in this poem as in others, is a footstep to an throne, for, as in "Love's Perfection,"

> Love may not, though it may have purely yearned,
> Lightly approach the mightily removed.

> For onward, ineradicably grooved,
> Go the splayed pathways of the heaven externed
> Till . . . spirit service in the body proved. (408)

The most poignant of Cousins' love poems for Gretta, "Bondage and Freedom," is in his last volume, *Twenty-Four Sonnets*. Cousins returns to his effective use of the paradox to strengthen the poem, which recalls his engagement to Gretta some forty years earlier.

> There is a rock that runs into the sea
> Under the changings of an Irish sky,
> And asks the gossiping waters, wandering by,
> What news they bring of that which is to be.
> And when she sat on the Ring Rock with me,
> Earth's question seemed to cloud her hazel eye:
> And on my lip hovered the sea's reply:
> "Love's bond shall set the aspiring spirit free."
>
> For on that day I placed on her left hand
> The ring that linked our lives, core within core;
> And on my body laid the soul's commands;
> While she to service vowed her garnered store.
> And now our hearts chant on a twilit strand:
> "Love that has set free has bound us more and more."[31]

The poignancy of the sonnet arises from intertwining the personal feeling, the unfolding of the event, the specific Irish setting, and the larger symbolic setting in calling up the concluding paradox. The use of the sea and Ring Rock as the background of the cherished moment of the past recalls the successful 1908 poem, "Slieve Cullen." The simplicity of the vocabulary and the statement in iambic pentameter provides directness of human encounter against the permanence of the rock and of the sea "under the changings of an Irish sky." After the octave's concluding statement, the sestet progresses to a wiser statement, a fitting paradox that brings together the moment of declaration of love in the past, and the present increase of devotion and uniting, seen with age and perspective with the sea and the rock enduring. The poem has a wistful melancholy and sadness that come as improving ingredients. Cousins' idealism is never lost, but the implied sorrow adds a mellow emotion that increases the poetry.

F. *Subject Matter: The Suffragette Movement*

There are also several lyric poems by James Cousins which stand apart from the others, the poems inspired by the suffragette movement. Cousins' interest in the movement for women's rights was, of course, highly personal, for not only did he support the actions of his wife Gretta, but he also passionately believed that the uplifting of women was a spiritual as well as social necessity. For as humanity was in reality a dual manifestation of the creative spirit progressing toward the ultimate apotheosis in the final eternal existence, the uniting of parallel if opposite sexes was essential.

The poems resulting from his commitment to the movement are extremely strong, passionate, and emphatic. While such terms as these rarely apply to Cousins' verse, here they can be used without impunity. They are apt terms for "Free as the Waves They Sang."

> "Free as the waves"—they sang—"the waves that
>   swell
> And break in large free laughter round her coasts,
> Is England!"—sang the dedicated hosts
> That, for her sake, went forth and bravely fell.
> But now a word, like some heart-breaking knell,
> Stirs with mute agony their solemn ghosts,
> For England—England that of freedom boasts—
> For Freedom's champions finds—a prison cell!
> Oh! cease your mocking, England, of the name
> Of Her whose face shall never bless your sight
> Till man and woman, sharing equal right,
> And linked in equal honor, equal shame,
> Move, as of old, twin orbs in God's clear light
> And purge the world with one unwavering flame.[32]

There is also a tone of haughty derision and mockery in this poem. Gone are the thoughtful calm, the classic restraint, the sensitive delicacy. In their place is a sputtering octave which almost loses control in its jagged haste. The last six lines are of poetic merit elsewhere unseen in Cousins, for the strength is still there and the control is returned and in one breathless sentence the point is made. Perhaps the presence of this vigor is so refreshing as to elevate the poem above its true worth, and perhaps the poem is too much of a political treatise, but it does stand forth among the poems of Cousins.

The other suffragette poems contain the same quality of force,

but none of them is as good as "Free as the Waves They Sang." "To
One in Prison" is addressed to Gretta, and sings her praise,

> Dear! on Love's altar thou hast laid thee down,
> Priestess and Victim of such Sacrifice
> As might melt praise from very hearts of ice,
> But wins the scoff of sycophant and clown.
> Yet in that band, whose glory is the frown
> Of sceptered tyranny and stained device,
> Thou hast a place; and thee it shall suffice
> To tread with them the path to high renown.[33]

It must also be noted that Cousins could be just as conventional
and ineffective when dealing with the subject of women's rights as
with other topics. In praising women for struggling toward destiny
and placing their shoulders to the cross, Cousins wrote these trite
lines:

> O fateful heralds, charged with Time's decree,
> Whose feet with doom have compassed Error's wall;
> Whose lips have blown the trump of Destiny
> Till ancient thrones are shaking toward their fall;
> Shout! for the Lord hath giv'n to you the free
> New age that comes with great new hope to all![34]

G. Tone and Vocabulary

His belief in a fundamental spiritual essence, evident in his verse,
regardless of subject matter, shapes the vocabulary, the tone, and
the poetic techniques of Cousins' shorter poems, no matter what the
form or subject. In the shorter poems, he developed disciplined control of various stanzaic patterns, including the Spenserian stanza
and the couplet. His experiments in line length ranged from a poem
in iambic dimeter, "Love in Absence,"[35] to a significant number of
poems with long lines of hexameter or septameter. Also, he
attempted some French forms suggested to him by James Stephens:
a rondel, "A Spring Rondel by a Starling," and a rondeau,
"Laborare est Orare."[36] These two poems are revealingly bad:
Cousins is not good at lightly delicate, quick line, as these lines indicate,

> I clink my castanet,
>   And beat my little drum
>   For spring at last has come,

> And on my parapet
> Of chestnut, gummy wet
>   Where bees begin to hum,
> I clink my castanet,
>   And beat my little drum.
>
>   "Spring goes," you say, "suns set."
>   So be it! Why be glum?
>   Enough, the spring has come;
> And without fear or fret
> I clink my castanet,
>   And beat my little drum.

The same inability is revealed in his attempts at iambic dimeter, as seen in these lines from "Love in Absence,"

> Long days that shine,
> Or richly weep;
> The dreamful mine
> Of happy sleep,
> Without thee, give
> A slender part:
> I need thy heart
> That life may live!
>
> Hear then my cry,
> And hasten, sweet!
> The world and I
> Are incomplete;
> Poor with all pelf;
> Bound most when freed:
> Thy Self I need,
> To be my Self![37]

The subject and tone in these lines are not suited to the dimeter line, and therein is suggested the limiting qualities of Cousins' talent. The subject and tone that is close to the central quality of Cousins is the thoughtful, the somewhat meditative, and the frequently elusive or shadowy internal uplift of emotional or spiritual speculation or dreamy flight. The dimeter line and the interesting rhyme scheme combination in the lines above are simply not in harmony with the plea of the words.

There is too much potential for speed in the short line and frequent rhyme. Cousins cannot put away his predilection for the profound, and hence these profundities become absurd when cast into the sing-song pattern. Cousins was unable to move with light speed in the form, nor could he freely use slow and elongated sounds and control the dimeter line length for his purposes. He could not observe the short line length to give greater emphasis to each final word.

In addition to "Love In Absence," Cousins also attempted the short line in a significant number of poems such as "Marguerite"[38] and "Sirius,"[39] each a poem with lines of one or two words and an attempt at succinct imagistic depictions. Consistently the conciseness and the concreteness are beyond Cousins' range. But the courage and seriousness of purpose Cousins displayed in this verse experimentation are praiseworthy.

He has greater success in the tetrameter or the pentameter line, or longer, with a rhythm that suits the style of his more typical abstracted or evanescent utterance, in lines that allow him to weave his abstracted realm, to evoke its delicacy, and to suggest its unifying eternal aspect. There are frequent passages of this kind in the narratives. An example in the short poems are these lines from "The Awakening":

> In this enchanted hour 'twixt light and light
> Of sinking moon and widening morn, mine ear
> Gathers from quivering leaf, and river clear,
> Sounds sweetened by the touch of passing Night;
> While on a leafy platform, shut from sight,
> But to the heart, by hearing, doubly near,
> A songbird, throbbing with the opening year,
> Outsoars in joy his wing's supremest flight.
>
> New day, new birth, new hope, new power have given
> Wings to the soul to soar, and leave behind
> Life's inessentials. What a majestic sky
> Is this where, unamazed, from some old heaven,
> I hear the Harp of Angus on the wind,
> And mark Cuchullin's Shade speed singing by?[40]

The kind of subject—the moonlight, enchantment, sweetness, and the heavenly comfort—and the soft mellowness of the vocabulary communicating a spiritual and meditative peace—both frequent in Cousins, are more aptly expressed in a longer, unfleeting line as they are here.

The abstract world that Cousins frequently rises to express often places demands on his control of his vocabulary. The demands are such that they frequently strain the vocabulary, so that Cousins' use of a single word becomes the breaking point which shatters the previously built delicacy; Cousins simply falters in word choice, as with the word *pelf* in the previously quoted "Love in Absence." And, since Cousins is often a "mood poet," whose meaning is implicit in the atmosphere he has created, the poor choice of a word can shatter an entire verse. This is true in this stanza; the word *pelf* destroys the stanza beyond recall. Since Cousins usually wants to define and clarify the supernatural essence of the natural realm, he is not satisfied solely with the creation of fantasy, of a region beyond realities of the present; he wants to present the melded unity of the tangible present with the eternal. His subject matter and word choice must not only be in present realities, but also must be clothed in eternal essences or infused with supernatural presence. The attempt at such an infusion leads to personified abstractions, in which the real quality, abstracted into personification, represents continuing and eternal essence.

Also, Cousins is led to a poetic vocabulary heightened beyond effectiveness, to "gleams from past the verge of sight" as in "Etain the Beloved," or as in this sestet from "Heaven and Earth,"

> O trembling tears of dawn in Nature's eyes!
> Forget your sadness: lo! the waited hour
> When recreant Love turns loveward, thrills the dome,
> Earth lifts mute praying hands in tree and flower,
> And Heaven in all the windows of the skies
> Hangs nightly lamps to light the wanderer home. [41]

This stanza cannot bear close scrutiny. No image is real; no personification is viable. It is merely a collection of words. The apostrophe to the "trembling tears," the very term "trembling tears," the exclamatory statements, the use of *lo!*, the phrase "thrills the dome," are all attempts at a heightened tone by resorting to poetic vocabulary and poetic contrivance. Indeed, the idea of Heaven hanging lamps in the windows of the sky is the most flagrant illustration of such striving for profundity. The result of this kind of attempt is usually a collection of worn clichés or weary doggerel in stereotyped rhythms, with the occasional lamentable addition of the precious ending, as in *oozy* and *skyey* in these lines which describe an angel raising himself from earth.

> About his feet the oozy clay
> Gripped fast, but could not stop or stay
> His course, till on his skyey stair
> He paused beyond the need for prayer,
> While from the air beneath, around,
> There rose a tumult of glad sound.[42]

Cousins' use of a "poetic" vocabulary reminds us that his verse is often very imitative or derivative: his idealisms are reminiscent of Shelley, his melodies of Tennyson. Self-taught in writing drama and poetry, he set himself poetic disciplines to accomplish. But such devoted study and dedication can have their drawbacks; Cousins' lines, though carefully made, often lack a distinctive poetic vitality.

H.   *Metaphor, Simile, and Paradox*

The task of expressing the unity of essence in the natural and the supernatural is admittedly a difficult one, for once external forms and shapes are perceived to be nonexistent or to meld into an amorphous whole, the language of concrete reality is inadequate and inappropriate. But Cousins discovered both a form and a poetic device that allowed his verse to stay in the present, yet deal in the eternal. The technique was the extended metaphor or simile, and this he developed into a skillfully-used formula. A stanza or section of a poem dealt with some realistic or natural entity; the next stanza or section, through comparison, drew the eternal or supernatural parallels.

The form Cousins found useful for this pattern was the sonnet, particularly the Petrarchan sonnet, which provided the natural octave-sestet division in which he could depict first the natural or concrete phenomena or reality, and then interpret it in ethereal terms in the second division. An early use of metaphor occurs in the lyric poem, "The Captive Butterfly," in *The Voice of One* in 1900, written in an attempt at an Irish meter in English. The first stanza reads,

> Thou lovely, light, and airy thing,
>   Flitting on wing from flower to flower
> Blossom and dew are thy bouquet brief,
>   Thyself but a leaf that lasts an hour.

The last stanza draws the butterfly as representative

> Of what my soul shall surely be,
>   When fully free from earth to rise,
> And flit among eternal flowers,
>   In fadeless bowers, 'neath cloudless skies.[43]

This pattern of comparison becomes the structural basis for the octave and sestet in the sonnet, "Love's Peace" (1906):

> Hushed with the mellow minstrelsy of rills
> That, on cool piney summits, laughing wake,
> And swan-like sing themselves away,—the lake,
> Like a soft eye, with quiet rapture fills;
> And of its fulness overflows, and thrills
> Seaward, to mingle where lovd billows break
> And tell, when tempests their harsh clamour make
> Of peace enfolded in these happy hills.
> So, love, may we from each exalted hour
> Go forth, with hearts filled full of quiet power
> That to the powerless hope and solace brings;
> And mingle with the world's tumultuous days
> Rumours of song by sunlit mossy ways,
> And peace that welleth at the heart of things.[44]

The octave limits its scenic description to the observable material details of the hills, the pines, the lake, and its streams running to the sea. The sestet draws the similarity of the two lovers to the scene, with the hope that together, filled with quiet power, they may go on their way to mingle with the sea-like body of "peace that welleth at the heart of things."

The realistic half of the comparison is frequently an element in nature, with a Romantic earthiness about it. In "Behind the Plough," those details are carefully developed in a homely metaphor:

> Black wings and white in the hollow
> Follow the track of the team,
> While the sun from the noon declining
> Is shining on toil-wet brows.
> Birds of the mountain and sea-birds
> Circle and swoop and scream,
> Searching for spoils of the furrow
> Where slowly the ploughman ploughs.

> Make me room, O birds! I am sweeping
> From the Boughs of Sleeping afar;
> I have winged thro' the mists of the ages,
> Where sages drone and drowse;
> I follow the feet of the Horses
> That drag the Morning Star,
> To search in the spoils of the furrow,
> Where God the Ploughman ploughs.[45]

Just as various birds follow the plough searching for any worms turned up with the earth, so too does Cousins, whose spirit is compared to a bird, search over the earth for spiritual food turned by God.

More successful is the simile with a familiar scene in the short poem, "At Streamstown, Connemara":

> From far-off peaks in summer drowned,
> The river rushed by you and me,
> And in an ecstasy of sound
> Leaped straight into the sea!
>
> With faith as firm, and equal mirth,
> May you and I, in time to be,
> Leap from our ledge of crumbling earth
> Into the Spirit's sea.[46]

The simile is obvious and directly stated in this relatively simple but successful poem, whose effectiveness is dependent upon the clarity of the simile, the regularity of the meter, and the uncomplicated stanzaic pattern. The poem's directness suggests Cousins' confidence in his firm faith and in the existence of the "Spirit's sea."

Having acquired control of his form and technique by thus separating the real and unreal, and allowing the real to represent or mirror the unreal, Cousins also became capable of mixing the two together. In the poem "Vision," for example, Cousins narrates the experience of excerpting from nature the meaning beneath the surface:

> When I from life's unrest had earned the grace
> Of either ease beside a quiet stream;
> When all that was, had mingled in a dream
> To eyes awakened out of time and place;

> Then in the cup of one great moment's space
> Was crushed the living wine from things that seem:
> I drank the joy of very Beauty's gleam,
> And saw God's glory face to shining face.
>
> Almost my brow was chastened to the ground,
> But for an inner Voice that said: "Arise!
> Wisdom is wisdom only to the wise:
> Thou art thyself the Royal thou hast crowned:
> In Beauty thine own beauty thou hast found,
> And thou hast looked on God with God's own eyes."[47]

Here the poet can be envisioned beside a stream, but that is not the true state of things, for the poet explains that his vision is now that of one who perceives rather than one who sees. The image of the grape and the wine is actually very good, and to a reader equipped with a knowledge of Cousins' philosophy, the juxtaposition of real and unreal in the line, "Then in the cup of one great moment's space," is appropriate, for a cup is definable and gives shape—but not limitation—to the overall image. And this is exactly what Cousins strives for in his attempt to describe the unreal in terms of the real: to give his ideas palpable meaning but not mundane and confining concreteness.

A similar uniting of visible and essential is present in "Slieve Cullen," but on a far more effective level.

> The dusk fell grey on Cullen
> When we climbed, my love and I.
> Like a dream the dim world faded,
> And the lovely stars drew nigh.
> Oh, our thoughts were full of labour,
> Weary limbs and shattered spears,
> While the face of Ireland darkened
> As it darkened thro' the years,
> Thro' the broken, bleeding years.
>
> The night lay deep on Cullen
> When we slept, my love and I,
> On the fragrant, whisp'ring heather,
> With our faces to the sky.
> Oh, our dreams were full of longing,
> Full of ancient woe and tears,
> While the heart of Ireland slumbered
> As it slumbered thro' the years,
> Thro' the slow and heavy years.

The dawn broke sweet on Cullen
When we woke, my love and I,
And the mists, like marching heroes,
Swiftly, silently went by.
Oh, we sent three shouts to heaven,
And we snapped the chain of fears,
For the soul of Ireland rises
To possess the coming years,
Rises, triumphs thro' the years![48]

Here the dreams are filled with human history and the hopes are for a perceivable goal—the freedom of a nation. The lovers are identifiable human beings, and the mountain is a geographical certainty (Sugar-loaf Mountain in County Wicklow). But at the same time the poem is set into a universal framework, and the forces of nature—the stars, the heather, and the mists—are emblematic of the centuries of past history. Even the lovers represent the idea of Ireland as they labor, as they slumber, and as they rise.

This is one of Cousins' best short poems. The sustained parallelism between Ireland and the lovers matches the sustained parallelism of form and wording within the stanzas themselves. The repetition of the idea of the final two lines of each stanza adds credence to the idea. The rhyme scheme effectively echoes the simplicity of the form. But more than any of these technical excellences, the poem is filled with sincere emotion, and one feels the sadness and the longing and the enthusiasm of the young man who loves his country and desires its good. And it is, surely, one of the most effective interweavings of the real and the ideal.

Another poem which achieves this mingling and also exhibits the patriotic stirrings is "High and Low."

He stumbled home from Clifden fair
With drunken song, and cheeks aglow.
Yet there was something in his air
That told of kingship long ago.
I sighed—and inly cried
With grief that one so high should fall so low.

He snatched a flower and sniffed its scent,
And waved it toward the sunset sky.
Some old sweet rapture thro' him went
And kindled in his bloodshot eye.

> I turned—and inly burned
> With joy that one so low should rise so high. [49]

It is in the drunken man himself that Cousins mixes his double vision of the ethereal and base capacities and makeup of man.
Notably, it is the drunken man's responsiveness to nature—the
flower he sniffs and the sunset he waves toward—that represent the
higher awarenesses. The poem also recalls Cousins' abhorrence of
alcohol, evident in his play, "'A Man's Foe."

It is perhaps somewhat unfortunate that this is the poem of
Cousins' that has been most frequently anthologized,[50] because
there are other poems that are more representative of his skill. But
the choice of subject—the common man in nature—and the fact
that Cousins was part of the Literary Renaissance make it seem an
obvious selection from the point of view of an anthology of the
Revival poets.

But somewhat typical in the poem is the savoring of paradox—the "low" man actually revealing "high" capacities—for very
often Cousins' approach to the theme of perceiving the quintessen-
tial in the phenomenal world leads him to the paradoxical nature of
human existence. His similes, comparisions, or metaphors therefore
often turn or twist at the end of the poem, as in "High and Low."
In the poem, "Love and Death," the paradox is the age-old one of
the defeat of death by the immortality of man's soul.

> Love lifts before the face of Death
> A passionate, imploring hand.
> "Oh! touch not my beloved" he saith,
> "Nor on his threshold stand."
> Death bent and kissed the face of Love,
> And said: "From life's loud hours that fleet
> In strife, thy love goes forth: the Dove
> Of peace is at my feet.
>
> I come to free him from the thrall
> Of life, and Life abundant give.
> Except a corn of wheat shall fall
> And die, it cannot live."
>
> Love looks upon the face of Death
> With eyes that see and understand.
> "Enter to my beloved", he saith,—
> And kissed Death's gentle hand. [51]

Here death is embraced at last by love as the harbinger of a greater life; indeed, of real life. Death is really life. And again, in the poem, "Ireland in Autumn," the merging and deceptiveness of death and life are the themes. The paradox which forms and develops throughout the poem is simply repudiated at the end. Once again, the overriding theme of Cousins—the interfusion of the real and the unreal—is seminal.

> Somewhat of Autumn's splendour round her lies;
> Yet think it not the prelude of her death,
> For there is that within her heart which saith
> The living word that blossoms in her eyes:
> "Heed not the portent of the season's skies,
> Nor dream the clouds more than a passing breath
> Sundrawn from half a world that offereth
> Its votive incense to the year that flies".
>
> The hand that bevels down the shortening day
> Is one with that which quickens leaf and wing,
> So prophecy of pregnance in decay
> Thou hast, and in thine Autumn, germs of spring
> To vindicate the lips that late have said:
> 'They dreamed a lie who dreamed thee wholly dead.'[52]

The subject of autumn, of course, suggests the coming of winter and death, but the opening lines caution the reader not to think of it as a prelude to Ireland's death. The season of autumn and its clouds represent only half of the reality of Ireland's existence. The other half is represented in the octave by the spring-like blossom in her eyes. The sestet talks of the energies preceding birth, which have "prophecy of pregnance," "germs of spring," and which quicken the leaves. The source of spring and of autumn is the same; the origin of life and of death is, paradoxically, the same. Hence, the seemingly dying Ireland is not dead, but is coming into life. The last four lines of "Ireland in Autumn" contain the same image as that of the preceding "Love and Death," for in the seed of Autumn lies the birth of Spring. Death breeds life. What appears to be the end is actually the beginning.

The consistency of Cousins' thought and utterance is quite remarkable. It yields unity to the body of his poetry. Perhaps nothing illustrates this more clearly than this simple, but lovely, six-line poem.

> Love dwells alone at Love's own fire,
> Nor otherwhere has ever moved:
> I am what I in thee desire,
> And thou, what thou in me has proved:
> Love's near is far, Love's distant nigh,
> Since I am thou, and thou are I.[53]

Although the sentiment herein expressed has long before been more cleverly stated by John Donne in "The Flea" and more beautifully stated by Donne in "The Ecstacy," this poem is a fitting representative of Cousins' lyric abilities, turning on paradox but delighting in synthesis, with Love the source, center, and agency of synthesis. The opposites in these lines are the two sexes, but the poem concludes that male is female and female is male when each is melted by love's fire into one. The love is near since it is in both people, but it is also far since it is an ethereal, cosmic force seemingly never moving from its own abode. But its abode is everywhere; it is infused in everything, including the man and the woman, who find a unifying similarity in the eternal love that unites them. The short poem is a fitting representative of Cousins' thought and ability: it focuses on paradox but rejoices in synthesis; it moves from the small and local to the cosmic; and it revolves about the metaphoric identification of the individual with the immense.

Thus, as in the longer poems, in the short poems was all subject matter shaped and expressed through his firmly held and unchanging Theosophical philosophy, built on the foundations of his own insights and intuition, and on his own and his wife's incursions into the realm of the living spirits or living consciousnesses of the next world. Myth was a presentation of spiritual origins, history, and prophecy; nature was the symbolic manifestation of the infinite; an individual location or event was commemorated, placed, or invested with its eternal perspective; love was celebrated reverently as preparation for the divine. In Cousins' verse, everything became part of an essential unity and synthesis of all things.

He wrote industriously in many established forms and meters, succeeding moderately in some. Using verse for the pronouncement of his world view, he frequently surmounted the difficulty of its expression by using the phenomenal world either to represent or mirror the noumenal world. Cousins continually saw the elements of existence with his own inner vision; this inner order was then imposed on what he saw, and this became the familiar expression of his poetic utterance, frequently with homely metaphors or attempts at heightening tangible reality to idealistic levels. Defective word choice often destroys an evanescent mood or an idealized view. While the rhythms are meticulously cared for, this kind of near perfection of regularity frequently becomes monotonous. The quanitity of verse is considerable, but its range and quality do not change. The essential vision of Cousins remains the same; the style and content of the verse, which is frequently unsubtle and facile, becomes repetitive, with a faltering straining for the assured ethereal vision, and an inability to face gloomy or disheartening realities of life. When Cousins faced his own death in one of his last poems, his sorrow added a somber tone and darkness previously absent in his verse. The sorrow was deepened by Cousins' knowledge of the deaths of Yeats and AE, and by the evident burial of each outside of Ireland. (Yeats' body had not then been returned from France to Sligo.) The poem, "Three Irish Poets," devotes a verse to each poet. With its direct statement, the abruptness of the short lines, and the incursion of gloom—with destiny's hand staggered and disorder jarring the stars—the poem has a sober effectiveness and an understandable sense of anxiety.

> I.   1867 - 1935
> What stagger in its hand
> Bewildered destiny
> So darkly that AE,
> Who walked with Irish Gods
> on holy Irish sods,
> Found death on Saxon land?
>   . . .
>
> II.   1865 - 1939
> And what disorder jars
> Fixed stars and wandering stars,
> That Yeats should lie alone
> Above Mentone.
>   . . .
>
> III.   1873 -
> Where will he die, the third
> Of that small singing clan
> Who heard the sacrificial word
> That frees the soul of man;
> He who from golden stuff and silver thread

> Through Celtic vision wrought
> Vedantic thought?
>
> . . .
> Where will his body lie
> When his day comes to die?[54]

Cousins was cremated in India on the day after he died, February 20, 1956.

CHAPTER 5

Conclusion

AS with so many Irish Writers, Cousins' life brought him away from Ireland. His early years in Belfast sent him on his spiritual journey away from the narrow religious view of his youth. His subsequent years in Dublin brought him toward a unifying view of a harmonized natural and spiritual existence, a dedication of many writers of the Revival, as indeed it was the idealistic drive of the modern political leaders of Ireland's struggle for independence. Through his imagination and Celtic mythology, Cousins found his own road to the universal spirit, and to beliefs defined and developed through his firm acceptance of Theosophy. What he had taken from his immersion in the Literary Revival became the idealistic vision that shaped totally the theme and form of his writings and his activities until his death in 1956. His interests never took him to investigation or penetration of the distinctiveness of the Celtic strain; his goal was to search out the unifying eternal through the Celtic legends. His desire to move among immortal themes is the foundation of his drama and verse; the desire is so strong, that seldom does he deal solely with merely human subject matter in human terms. Perhaps it is therefore ironic that his very few incursions into the human realm seem to be the more successful of his poems. The idealistic heightening is always present, sometimes in strained emotionalizing and sentimentality, or in awkward or homely metaphors. When Cousins succeeds, his verse creates a delicate world, abstracted from earthly reality, suspended enchantingly at the doors of an alluring heaven. Such a realm is a frail one, and easily blasted by a clumsy word or an awkward rhyme; a wistful felicitousness and a soft euphony are essentials that frequently elude Cousins.

He held to his idealism as strongly as Shelley, and for many more years; his idealism shaped his actions as well as his literary works. While the Orient and Oriental philosophies were a strong attraction to Yeats and Russell and other early writers of the Revival, only Cousins acted on that attraction and made that spiritual source his actual home. His years in India, with their wide range of cultural activities, his acceptance into Hindu worship, his firm vege-tarianism, were actions in the earthly realm aimed at moving forward and upward the world of men to the inevitable perfection of the gods of man's origin, before and beyond the earthly manifestation. His successful marriage united him with a vital woman who shared his Theosophical beliefs and who herself was ac-tive in her efforts to make real her ideals, just as Cousins worked to make real his ideals in his activities and in his verse and drama.

Cousins' role in the origins and development of Irish drama in bringing together George Russell and the Fay brothers, and in writing his two early plays, *The Sleep of the King* and his best play, *The Racing Lug*, earn him a significant place in the history of Irish drama—that major efflorescence of the Irish Literary Revival. His plays, with their inherent poetic lyricism, are representative of the evanescent idealism of the early works of the Revival, before the in-trusions of the realism of Synge and O'Casey. His inabilities with realism, however, work to diminish his artistic value in the dramatic movement in Ireland, though his place in the Revival is secure on historical grounds. His idealisms, isolated as they are from elements of realism, are more poetic pageantry than drama. The certainty and the narrowness of his view, among other things, prevented him from writing plays with sustaining dramatic interest and effec-tiveness. The significance of Cousins' plays is as period pieces.

While his drama is of value in literary history, the verse, which spanned the years in Ireland and in India, is more central to Cousins' talent, and of more inherent literary worth. There are lyrics and narratives in a variety of complex forms, rhythms, and meters, displaying careful workmanship and discipline in poetic craft. The better short poems, such as "Slieve Cullen" and the sonnet, "Vision," show a responsiveness to nature, an idealism, and a love of country. The verse of value reveals a sensitivity and delicacy of description, invested with supernatural meaning in a cosmic perspective. It is here that Cousins' major value and significance lie, as a poet giving lyrical voice to the Theosophical point of view, a view that reveals itself throughout some of the ma-jor literary work of the Irish Literary Renaissance, a view that is a part of the broader Celtic vision of an existence made up of the natural and the supernatural. Cousins' own expanding personal spiritual consciousness brought him to investigate and interpret the Celtic myths in his own way, and while he never penetrated or presented the national consciousness in works, as Yeats and Synge may be said to have done, he evolved his own harmonizing vision of being, his own set of beliefs through the Celtic myths as a form of spiritual symbolism bridging the ages. The mythological narrative, notably "Etain the Beloved," is best suited to Cousins' talent and interest. There, he can and does present his personal Theosophical view of the cosmos and man's place therein in verse of delicate and otherworldly lyricism, telling events that suggest a philosophy which unites all men, West and East, and all things, real and spiritual. The verse, like the drama, has significance in literary history, but it also has an artistic quality that qualifies it as significant and revealing poetry coming from the Literary Renaissance in Ireland, and, in a broader view, testifying again to the idealistic aspirations of humanity as it continues to attempt to assure itself of a supernatural mission in a spiritual universe.

The failure of Cousins to become a major author is at least in part the result of his self-satisfied narrowness of view. It is strange to conclude that of a man whose philosophy was so unconfined, but he clung so tenaciously to the comfortable beliefs he discovered in his earlier years that everything was funneled into his preconceived framework. Cousins' critical insight into the poetry of George Russell—that it had the "peculiar feature as of a preconcerted movement in one direction, as though its trees were bending always westward before a wind which blows ever from the East"—could justifiably apply to Cousins' writings. As a result, his writing is static. Nothing really *happens*. There is merely the narration of events, the illustration of points, the explication of a point of view. There is never tension or discovery; there is no passion; there is no challenge. There is, however, order, skill, control, lyric delicacy, and sporadically expanding loveliness.

Notes and References

Chapter One

1. James H. and Margaret E. Cousins, *We Two Together* (Madras, 1950), p. 3. Page numbers for future references are given in parentheses in the text.
2. *A Wandering Harp* (New York, 1932), p. vi.
3. Richard Ellman, *James Joyce* (London, 1959), p. 256n.
4. *Joseph Holloway's Abbey Theatre: A Selection from His Unpublished Journal*, ed. Robert Hogan and Michael J. O'Neill (Carbondale, Illinois, 1967), p. 40.
5. Ellman, *James Joyce*, p. 168.
6. *Ibid.*, p. 177.
7. Ernest Boyd, *The Contemporary Drama of Ireland* (Boston, 1917), p. 116.
8. Boyd, p. 121.
9. *The Letters of W. B. Yeats*, ed. Allan Wade (London, 1954), p. 372.
10. *Ibid.*, p. 379.
11. *Ibid.*, p. 417.
12. Abindrath Chandra Bose, *Three Mystic Poets: A Study of W. B. Yeats, A.E., and Rabindranath Tagore*, intro. James H. Cousins (Kolhapur, Madras, 1945), pp. vi - vii.
13. Rabindranath Tagore, *Gitanjali, Collected Poems and Plays* (London, Macmillan Co., 1936), p. 16.
14. "The Cousins Presentations," *Irish Citizen*, 2, No. 3, (7 June 1913), 20, col. 3.
15. *A Wandering Harp*, p. v - vi.

Chapter Two

1. L. W. Rogers, *Elementary Theosophy* (Wheaton, Illinois, Theosophical Press, 1929), p. 4.
2. *The Bases of Theosophy: A Study in Fundamentals, Philosophical, Psychological, Practical* (Madras, 1913), p. 14.
3. *Ibid.*, p. 21.
4. *Ibid.*, p. 25.
5. *The Renaissance in India* (Madras, 1918), p. 236.
6. George Russell, *The National Being* (Dublin, 1917), pp. 159 - 63.
7. *The Living Torch*, ed. Monk Gibbon (New York, 1938), p. 50.
8. *Ibid.*, pp. 13 - 14.

9.   *A Wandering Harp* (New York, 1932), p. v - vi.

10.   *The Wisdom of the West* (London, 1912), p. 19. Page numbers for future references are given in parentheses in the text.

11.   "Art and Irish Mythological Literature," *The Pioneer*, 1, No. 2 (March 1911), 62.

12.   *The Wisdom of the West*, p. 16.

13.   *War: A Theosophical View* (London, 1914), p. 14. Page numbers for future references are given in parentheses in the text.

14.   *Letters from AE*, ed. Alan   Denson (London, Abelard-Schuman 1961), p. 211.

15.   *We Two Together*, p. 467.

16.   *A Study in Synthesis* (Madras, 1934), p. vii. Page numbers for future references are given in parentheses in the text.

17.   *We Two Together*, p. 469.

18.   *The Kingdom of Youth: Essays Towards National Education* (Madras, 1917), p. 35. Page numbers for future references are given in parentheses in the text.

19.   *The Faith of the Artist* (Madras, 1941), p. viii. Page numbers for future references are given in parentheses in the text.

20.   *Work and Worship* (Madras, 1922), p. 30.

21.   *Ibid.*, p. 79.

22.   *Ibid.*, p. 96.

23.   *The Renaissance in India*, p. 162.

24.   *Ibid.*, p. 161.

25.   *Ibid.*, p. 164.

26.   *The Cultural Unity of Asia* (Madras, 1922).

27.   "Art and Criticism," *United Irishman*, 10, No. 227 (4 July 1903), 2.

28.   "Concerning Indications and Modern Irish Poetry," *The Pioneer*, 1, No. 1 (February 1911), p. 6.

29.   Joseph Holloway, *Impressions of a Dublin Playgoer*. Manuscript 1801 (Dublin, National Library of Ireland), 8 January 1903, p. 8.

30.   "Mysticism in English Poetry," *The Shanachie*, II, No. VI (Winter 1907), p. 212.

31.   *Ibid.*, p. 219.

32.   *The Renaissance in India*, pp. 204 - 05.

33.   *Ibid.*, pp. 202 - 03.

34.   *Ibid.*, pp. 288 - 89.

35.   *Footsteps of Freedom* (Madras, 1919), p. 5.

36.   *Modern English Poetry: Its Characteristics and Tendencies* (Madras, 1921), p. 91.

37.   *News Ways in English Literature* (Madras, 1917), p. 37.

Chapter Three

1.   "The Clansmen: An Irish Historical Play in Four Acts," *United Irishman*, 18 March 1905, p. 2.

2. "The Clansmen," *United Irishman*, 25 March 1905, p. 3.

3. "The Clansmen," *United Irishman*, 1 April 1905, p. 3.

4. *Ibid.*, p. 3.

5. "The Sleep of the King," *The Quest*, pp. 15 - 26. Page numbers for future references are given in parentheses in the text.

6. P. W. Joyce, *Old Celtic Romances* (London, 1879), pp. 74 - 78.

7. *We Two Together*, p. 73.

8. *Freeman's Journal*, 30 October 1902, p. 5.

9. *Daily Express*, 30 October 1902, p. 6.

10. *Freeman's Journal*, 30 October 1902, p. 5.

11. "The Sword of Dermot," *United Irishman*, 9, No. 218 (2 May 1903), 2. Page numbers for future references are given in parentheses in the text.

12. See "Letters," *All Ireland Review*, IV, No. 12 (25 April 1903), 138.

13. Holloway, *Impressions of a Dublin Playgoer*, Mss. 1801, 20 April 1903, p. 208.

14. In *Shama'a* (Madras), 7, Nos. 3 - 4 (July - October 1927), 153 - 76.

15. *Freeman's Journal*, 4 November 1903, p. 5.

16. *United Irishman*, 14 November 1903, p. 2.

17. "Sold: A Comedy of Real Life in Two Acts," *United Irishman*, 8, No. 200 (27 December 1902), 5 - 7.

18. *The Cork Constitution*, 27 December 1905, p. 4.

19. "The Turn of the Tide: A Play of Real Life in One Act," *United Irishman*, 26 August 1905, pp. 6 - 7; 2 September 1905, pp. 6 - 7.

20. "The Racing Lug," *United Irishman*, 5 July 1902, p. 3. Also in *Lost Plays of the Irish Renaissance*, ed. Robert Hogan and James Kilroy (Dixon, California, 1970), pp. 39 - 49.

21. Lady Gregory, *Our Irish Theatre* (New York, 1913), p. 101.

22. *Joseph Holloway's Abbey Theatre* (Carbondale, Illinois, 1967), p. 77.

23. *Shama'a*, 7, No. 3 - 4 (July - October 1927), 153 - 76.

24. *The King's Wife* (Madras, 1919). Also in Cousins, *A Bardic Pilgrimage: Second Selection of the Poetry* (New York, 1934), pp. 106 - 64; page numbers for future references are given from this volume, in parentheses in the text.

25. *The Hound of Uladh* (Madras, 1942), pp. 67 - 271. Page numbers for future references are given in parentheses in the text.

26. *We Two Together*, p. 568.

27. *Three Mystic Poets*, p. viii.

28. "Bricriu-Bitter-Tongue," *The Scholar*, XI, No. 2 - 3 (1935), 101 - 16.

29. *Wisdom of the West*, pp. 55 - 57.

30. *The Play of Brahma: An Essay on the Drama in National Revival* (Bangalore City, 1921), p. 10. Page numbers for future references are given in the text.

Chapter Four

1.   *Ben Madighan and Other Poems* (Belfast, 1894), p. 22. Page numbers for future references are given in parentheses in the text.
2.   *The Legend of the Blemished King and Other Poems,* The Little Library, Vol. 2, ed. M. J. Keats (Dublin, 1897), p. 26. Page numbers for future references are given in parentheses in the text.
3.   *The Quest* (Dublin, 1906), p. 4. Page numbers for future references are given in parentheses in the text.
4.   Standish O'Grady, *The Story of Ireland* (London, 1894), p. 6.
5.   *Sinn Fein,* 25 May 1907, p. 3.
6.   *We Two Together,* p. 218.
7.   H. d'Arbois de Jubainville, *The Irish Mythological Cycle and Celtic Mythology* (Dublin, Hodges & Figgis, 1903), pp. 176 - 82. Page numbers for future references are given in parentheses in the text.
8.   *We Two Together,* p. 210.
9.   *Etain the Beloved* (Dublin, 1912), p. 39. Page numbers for future references are given in parentheses in the text.
10.   Mary C. Sturgeon, *Studies in Contemporary Poets* (London, 1916), p. 27.
11.   *Collected Poems* (Madras, 1940), p. ix.
12.   *Three Mystic Poets,* p. iii.
13.   *The Story of Etain: A Celtic Myth and an Interpretation* (Dublin, 1925).
14.   *The Voice of One* (London, 1900), p. 9.
15.   *Three Mystic Poets,* p. viii.
16.   *We Two Together,* p. 678.
17.   *The Bell-Branch* (Dublin, 1908), p. 45. Page numbers for future references are given in parentheses in the text.
18.   *The Quest,* p. 49.
19.   "Vision," *The Awakening* (Dublin, 1907), n.pag.
20.   "Resurrection," *The Bell-Branch,* p. 12.
21.   *The Bell-Branch,* p. 25.
22.   *Collected Poems* (Madras, 1940), pp. 238 - 39. Since individual volumes of Cousins' verse published in India are not readily available, it is logical to refer to the *Collected Poems* for the verse written in India. Page numbers for future references are given in parentheses in the text.
23.   *The Bell-Branch,* p. 31.
24.   *Etain the Beloved,* pp. 56 - 57.
25.   *The Bell-Branch,* p. 65 and p. 42 respectively.
26.   *Ibid.,* p. 9.
27.   *Ibid.,* p. 31.
28.   *Ibid.,* p. 30.
29.   *The Awakening,* n.pag.
30.   *We Two Together,* p. 698.

31. *Twenty-Four Sonnets* (Madras, 1949), p. 21.
32. *The Bell-Branch*, p. 36.
33. *Etain the Beloved*, p. 80.
34. "Who Sets Her Shoulder to the Cross of Christ," *The Bell-Branch*, p. 35.
35. *Etain the Beloved*, pp. 58 - 59.
36. *Ibid.*, pp. 63 - 65.
37. *Ibid.*, pp. 58 - 59.
38. *The Bell-Branch*, p. 24.
39. *The Quest*, pp. 53 - 54.
40. *The Awakening*, n.pag.
41. *The Voice of One*, pp. 41 - 42.
42. "How the Mountains Came to Be," *Etain the Beloved*, p. 57.
43. *The Voice of One*, pp. 41 - 42.
44. *The Awakening*, n.pag.
45. *The Bell-Branch*, p. 9.
46. *Ibid.*, p. 16.
47. *The Awakening*, n.pag.
48. *The Bell-Branch*, p. 32.
49. *Ibid.*, p. 26.
50. In *Mentor Book of Irish Poetry*, ed. Devin Garrity (New York, 1965) are "High and Low," "Omens," "A Curse on a Closed Gate," pp. 86 - 87; in *1000 Years of Irish Poetry*, ed. Kathleen Hoagland (New York, 1949) are "Omens," "High and Low," "The Corncrake," pp. 631 - 32; in *Oxford Book of English Mystical Verse*, ed. D. H. S. Nicholson and A. H. E. Lee (Oxford, 1916) are "The Quest," "Vision," pp. 484 - 85; in *Oxford Book of Mystical Verse: XVII-XX Centuries*, ed. Donagh McDonagh and Lennox Robinson (Oxford, 1958), are "High and Low" and "Behind the Plough," pp. 160 - 61; in *Dublin Book of Irish Verse: 1728 - 1909*, ed. John Cooke (Dublin, 1909) are "The Coming of Niamh," "The Bell-Branch," "Behind the Plough," and "The Awakening," pp. 601 - 03.
51. *The Bell-Branch*, p. 27.
52. *The Legend of the Blemished King*, p. 93.
53. "Love Dwells Alone," *The Bell-Branch*, p. 22.
54. *Reflections Before Sunset* (Madras, 1946), pp. 35 - 37.

Selected Bibliography

PRIMARY SOURCES

Above the Rainbow and Other Poems. Madras: Ganesh and Co., 1926.
The Aesthetical Necessity in Life. Allahadad: Allahadad Law Journal Press, 1944.
"Art and Criticism," *United Irishman*, 10, No. 227 (4 July 1903), 2 - 3.
"Art and Irish Mythological Literature," *The Pioneer*, 1, No. 2 (mid-March, 1911), 59 - 63.
The Awakening and Other Sonnets. Dublin: Maunsel and Co., 1907.
A Bardic Pilgrimage. New York: Roerich Museum Press, 1934.
The Bases of Theosophy. Madras: Theosophical Publishing House, 1913.
The Bell Branch. Dublin: Maunsel and Co., 1908.
Ben Madighan and Other Poems. Belfast: Marcus Ward and Co., 1894.
"The Clansmen: An Irish Historical Play in Four Acts," *United Irishman*.
Act I (18 March 1905), pp. 2 - 3; Act II (25 March 1905), p. 3; Act III (1 April 1905), p. 3; Act IV (8 April 1905), p. 2.
Collected Poems (1894 - 1940). Madras: Kalakshetra, 1940.
"Concerning Indications and Modern Irish Poetry," *The Pioneer*, 1, No. 1 (mid-February, 1911), 3 - 7.
The Cultural Unity of Asia. Madras: Theosophical Publishing House, 1922.
"Eastern Thought and Western Theology," *The Pioneer*, 1, No. 3 (mid-April, 1911), 109 - 13.
Etain the Beloved. Dublin: Maunsel and Co., 1912.
The Faith of the Artist. Madras: Vasanta Press, 1941.
Footsteps of Freedom. Madras: Ganesh and Co., 1919.
Forest Meditation and Other Poems. Madras: Theosophical Publishing House, 1925.
The Fulfillment of Beauty. Calcutta: Swami Vireswarananda Art Press, 1938.
The Garland of Life: Poems West and East. Madras: Ganesh and Co., 1917.
The Girdle. Madras: Ganesh and Co., 1929.
Heathen Essays. Madras: Ganesh and Co., 1925.
The Hound of Uladh: Two Plays in Verse. Madras: Vasanta Press, 1942.
"Ibsen in Dublin," *Irish Citizen*, 1, No. 30 (14 December 1912), 238.
The Kingdom of Youth: Essays Towards National Education. Madras: Ganesh and Co., 1917.
The King's Wife. Madras: Ganesh and Co., 1919.

The Legend of the Blemished King and Other Poems. Dublin: Bernard Doyle, 1897.

"Letter," *All Ireland Review,* IV, No. 2 (25 April 1903), 138 - 39.

Modern English Poetry: Its Characteristics and Tendencies. Madras: Ganesh and Co., 1921.

A Modern Geography for Inter-Mediate Schools. Dublin: Maunsel and Co., 1909.

Moulted Feathers. Madras: Ganesh and Co., 1919.

"Mysticism in English Poetry," *The Shanachie,* II, No. VI (Winter 1907), 211 - 18.

The New Japan. Madras: Ganesh and Co., 1923.

New Ways in English Literature. Madras: Ganesh and Co., 1917.

Ode to Truth. Madras: Ganesh and Co., 1919.

The Oracle and Other Poems. Madras: Ganesh and Co., 1938.

The Play of Brahma: An Essay on the Drama in National Revival. Bangalore City: Amateur Dramatic Association, 1921.

"A Psychological Moment and Its Consequences," *Irish Citizen,* I, No. 52 (17 May 1913), 411.

The Quest. Dublin: Maunsel and Co., 1906.

"The Racing Lug," *United Irishman,* 8, No. 175 (5 July 1902), 3.

Reflections Before Sunset. Madras: Thompson and Co., 1946.

The Renaissance in India. Madras: Ganesh and Co., 1918.

Samadarsana: A Study in Indian Psychology. Madras: Ganesh and Co., 1925.

Sea-Change. Madras: Ganesh and Co., 1920.

The Shrine and Other Poems. Madras: Ganesh and Co., 1938.

"The Sleep of the King" and "The Sword of Dermot," William Feeney, ed., intro. William A. Dumbleton. Vol. VIII: The Irish Drama Series. Chicago: DePaul University, 1973.

"The Sleeptime Departed, A Lay Homily," *Irish Citizen,* 2, No. 32 (3 January 1914), 261.

"Sold: A Comedy of Real Life in Two Acts," *United Irishman,* 8, No. 200 (27 December 1902), 5 - 7.

The Story of Etain: A Celtic Myth and an Interpretation. Reprinted from *Theosophy in Ireland,* 1925.

Straight and Crooked. London: Grant Richards Ltd., 1915.

A Study in Synthesis. Madras: Ganesh and Co., 1934.

Sung by Six, with S. K. Cowan, W. M. Knox, L. J. McQuilland, W. T. Anderson, J. J. Pender. Belfast: R. Aickin and Co., 1896.

Surya-Gita. Madras: Ganesh and Co., 1922.

"The Sword of Dermot," *United Irishman,* 9, No. 218 (2 May 1903), 2 - 3.

The Sword of Dermot. Madras: Shama'a Publishing House, 1927.

Three Mystic Poets by Abinash Chandra Bose, with intro. by J. H. Cousins. Kolhapur, India: School and College Bookstall, 1945.

A Tibetan Banner and Other Poems. Madras: Ganesh and Co., 1926.
"The Turn of the Tide: A Play of Real Life in One Act," *United Irishman*
    (26 August 1905), pp. 6 - 7; (2 September 1905) pp. 6 - 7.
Twenty-four Sonnets. Madras: Kalakshetra, 1949.
Two Ways to Wisdom. Madras: Theosophical Publishing House, 1927.
The Voice of One. London: T. Fisher Unwin, 1900.
A Wandering Harp: Selected Poems. New York: Roerich Museum Press,
    1932.
War: A Theosophical View. London: Theosophical Publishing House, 1914.
"War and Superwar," *Irish Citizen*, 4, No. 18 (18 September 1915), 96 - 97.
We Two Together with Margaret E. Cousins. Madras: Ganesh and Co.,
    1950.
The Wisdom of the West. London: Theosophical Publishing Society, 1912.
Work and Worship: Essays on Culture and Creative Art. Madras: Ganesh
    and Co., 1922.
*The Work Promethean: Interpretations and Applications of Shelley's
    Poetry*. Madras: Ganesh and Co., 1933.

SECONDARY SOURCES

There has been little or no critical assessment of Cousins' work or of his role
in the Irish Literary Revival. There is no previous critical volume. Cousins'
plays and poems were reviewed by his contemporaries, as this listing shows.

BENET, WILLIAM ROSE. "Irish Poet from India," *Saturday Review of
    Literature*, 8 (4 June 1932), 772. Discusses Cousins on occasion of his
    visit to New York City.
BIGGAR, F. J. *Ulster Journal of Archaeology*, I, Part 1 (September 1894), 76.
    Rev. of *Ben Madighan*.
The Bookman, 42, Spring Supplement (April 1912), 25. Rev. of *Etain the
    Beloved*.
BOYD, ERNEST. *The Contemporary Drama of Ireland*. Boston: Little, Brown
    and Co., 1917. An early critical survey of Irish drama.
BOYD, ERNEST. *Ireland's Literary Renaissance*. Dublin: Maunsel and Co.,
    1916. A helpful early, and now somewhat outdated, discussion of
    growth of the Literary Movement.
"Cousins Presentation," *Irish Citizen*, 2, No. 3 (7 June 1913), 20 - 21. A
    report on the evening commemorating the Cousins' departure from
    Ireland for India.
CUGUAN. *United Irishman* (14 November 1903), p. 2. Rev. of "A Man's
    Foes."
CURTIS, W. O. L. *Sinn Fein* (27 February 1909), p. 3. Rev. of *The Bell
    Branch*.
Daily Express (30 October 1902), p. 6. Rev. of "The Sleep of the King."

DENSON, ALAN. *James Cousins and Margaret E. Cousins: A Bio-Bibliographical Survey*. Kendal, Westmoreland, England: published by compiler, 1967. An essential survey of the Cousins' works and activities.

ELLIS-FERMOR, UNA. *The Irish Dramatic Movement*. London: Methuen and Co., 1954. A helpful discussion of the principles and the development of theater in Ireland.

ELLMAN, RICHARD. *James Joyce*. London: Oxford University Press, 1959. A thorough and admirable life, touching on Joyce's relationship with Cousins.

FAY, W. G. and CATHERINE CARSWELL. *The Fays of the Abbey Theatre*. London: Rich and Cowan Ltd., 1935. A tracing of the Fay brothers' work, in which Cousins helped in establishing Irish drama.

Freeman's Journal (30 October 1902), p. 5. Rev. of "The Sleep of the King."

The Golden Book of Tagore: A Homage to Rabindranath Tagore from India and the World. Calcutta: Golden Book Co., 1931. A collection of works of the poet strongly admired by Cousins.

GREGORY, LADY AUGUSTA. *Our Irish Theatre*. New York: Putnam and Co., 1913. A presentation of the early principles at work in early Irish theater.

HOLLOWAY, JOSEPH. *Impressions of a Dublin Playgoer*. Manuscripts in National Library of Ireland, Dublin.
  Joseph Holloway's Abbey Theatre: A Selection from His Unpublished Journal, ed. Robert Hogan and Michael J. O'Neill. Carbondale: Southern Illinois University Press, 1967. The careful and astute insights from the diaries and journals of inveterate theatergoer in Dublin in the early part of the twentieth century.

Irish Citizen, 5, No. 56 (March 1918), 603. Rev. of *New Ways in English Literature*.

Irish Homestead, 15, No. 4 (25 January 1908), 77. Rev. of *The Awakening*.

Irish Times (29 March 1912), p. 9. Rev. of *Etain the Beloved*.

JOYCE, JAMES. *Letters of James Joyce*, ed. Richard Ellman. London: Faber and Co., 1966. Contains references to Cousins by Joyce.

JOYCE, P. W. *Old Celtic Romances*. London: David Nutt, 1879. A source for Celtic stories used by Cousins and other contemporary writers.

KEOHLER, THOMAS. *Sinn Fein* (23 March 1912), p. 2. Rev. of *Etain the Beloved*.

Living Torch: A.E., ed. Monk Gibbon. New York: Macmillan Co., 1938. An edition of selected writings of AE by his friend, with a useful introduction.

"A Loss to Irish Citizenship," *Irish Citizen*, 1, No. 41 (1 March 1913), 324. A tribute to Cousins at the time of his leaving Ireland for India.

Lost Plays of the Irish Renaissance, ed. Robert Hogan and James Kilroy. Dixon, California: Proscenium Press, 1970. Contains Cousins' sea play, *The Racing Lug.*

MAC CONNELL, BERNARD. *United Irishman,* 8, No. 193 (8 November 1902), 3. Rev. of *The Racing Lug.*

"Mananan." *Hermes,* No. 1 (February 1907), pp. 31 - 32. Rev. of *The Quest.*

MEAD, G. R. S. *The Theosophical Review,* X41, No. 247 (March 1908), 85. Rev. of *The Awakening.*

Mentor Book of Irish Poetry, ed. Devin A. Garrity. New York: New American Library, 1965. A broad selection of representative Irish verse.

NIC SHUIBHLAIGH, MAIRE. *The Splendid Years.* Dublin: James F. Duffy and Co., 1955. A discussion of the Irish theater by an actress in many of its plays.

O'CONGAILE, SEUMAS. *Sinn Fein* (25 May 1907), p. 3. Rev. of *The Quest.*

O'GRADY, STANDISH. *The Story of Ireland.* London: Methuen and Co., 1894. A book on Ireland and its history told in a vivid style; the book was an inspiration to authors early in the Celtic Revival.

Oxford Book of Irish Verse: XVIIth Century-XXth Century, ed. Donagh McDonagh and Lennox Robinson. Oxford: Clarendon Press, 1958. Contains two of Cousins' poems.

RUSSELL, GEORGE. *Letters from AE,* ed. Alan Denson. London: Abelard-Shuman, 1961. An interesting collection of letters by AE, who was a friend of, and influence upon, Cousins.

RUSSELL, GEORGE. *The National Being.* Dublin: Maunsel and Co., 1917. An influential book presenting the political idealism underlying the Irish struggle for independence.

STEPHENS, JAMES, *Irish Review,* 2, No. 14 (April 1912), 100 - 02. Rev. of *Wisdom of the West.*

STURGEON, MARY C. *Studies in Contemporary Poets.* London: George Harrap, 1916. Treats Cousins favorably in passing.

Times Literary Supplement (29 August 1912), p. 337. Rev. of *Etain the Beloved.*

Times Literary Supplement (3 January 1918), p. 10. Rev. of *New Ways in English Literature.*

Times Literary Supplement (28 August 1919), p. 463. Rev. of *Footsteps of Freedom.*

Times Literary Supplement (30 December 1920), p. 894. Rev. of *Sea-Change.*

Times Literary Supplement (8 December 1921), p. 831. Rev. of *Moulted Feathers.*

Ulster Journal of Archaeology, 3, Part 4 (July 1897), 279. Rev. of *The Legend of the Blemished King.*

Weekly Irish Times (11 January 1908), p. 18, Rev. of *The Awakening*.

WILKINS, MAURICE. *Irish Review*, 2, No. 17 (July 1912), 276 - 78. Rev. of *Etain the Beloved*.

1000 Years of Irish Poetry, ed. Kathleen Hoagland. New York: Grosset and Dunlap, 1949. Contains three of Cousins' poems.

YEATS, WILLIAM BUTLER. *The Letters of W. B. Yeats*, ed. Alan Wade. London: Rupert Hart-Davis, 1954. Contains letters showing Yeats' early enthusiasm for Cousins' work and his later distaste for it.

Index